THE
CRYSTAL
WORKSHOP

THE
CRYSTAL
WORKSHOP

A JOURNEY INTO THE HEALING
POWER OF CRYSTALS

AZALEA LEE

ARTISAN | NEW YORK

Dedicated to all
who wish to work with
the crystal beings in
sincerity, integrity, and love

CONTENTS

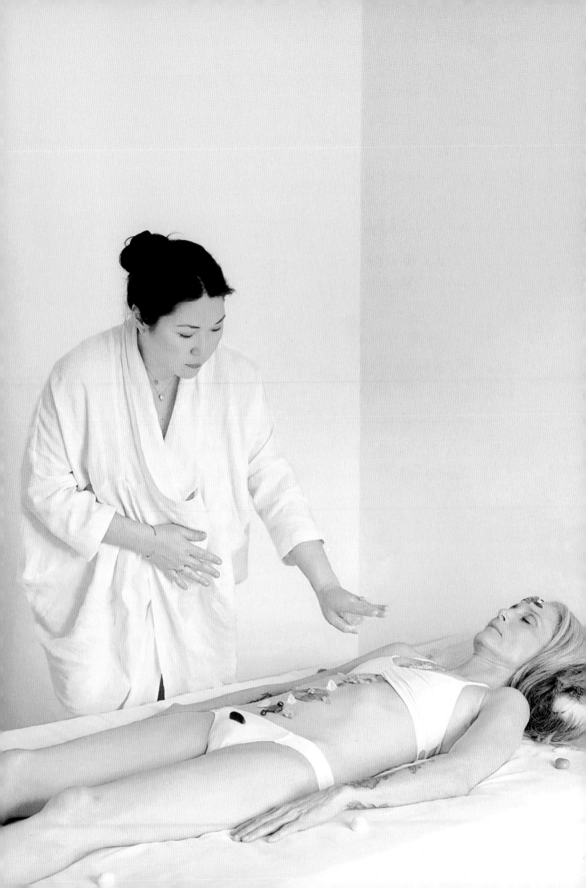

PREFACE

A CRYSTAL HEALER'S JOURNEY

I HAVE ALWAYS KNOWN I had come into the world for a purpose, but for what, I did not know. As a small child, I prayed to the Universe to tell me what I was supposed to do, for I could not shake the feeling that I was here to do *something*. Because of this persistent feeling, finding my calling became my utmost concern. My dreams did not include getting married or starting a family but were about solving the riddle of this yearning I had inside of me. Nothing was more important to me than discovering my purpose and giving my life to it.

I knew that my teenage years were supposed to be a time of discovery in all ways, but I still worried that I had no idea in what direction I was supposed to go. I became even more concerned when I was about to begin college, for I did not feel I was getting any guidance or opinion from the Universe. There were plenty of subjects that interested me, each leading to its own trajectory of a career, but as desperate as I was to begin on a path toward something, within me was an insistent pull that kept me from fully committing to anything but my purpose.

Life delayed my finishing college but, still seemingly without any sign of what I was supposed to be doing with my life, when I returned to school, I decided to major in film. Since film was a medium of stories, and stories had great power to heal, I surmised, perhaps, this might be my purpose. After graduating it seemed providential that I began immediately working with people whom I had long admired, so I thought I had been given the sign that I was on the right path to discover my life's purpose— and maybe that purpose was to share stories that healed.

But it felt as if the Universe was conspiring against me. My personal life kept thwarting any energy I put toward making my own stories to share, and the years were starting to roll by. Now in my thirties, I found myself working in costume design. I had unexpectedly met and married the love of my life. I fulfilled a dream of a home full of happy critters. It was wonderful, but that feeling I was born with still wouldn't leave me . . . *just what was I supposed to be doing?*

Working in costume design didn't feel like my purpose, and after so many years, making films didn't quite feel like it either. As much as I implored and begged the Universe to tell me, as much as I was still chomping at the bit to devote my life to my purpose, as much as I was willing to do whatever was asked of me, the Universe continued to remain mum.

Though I had been a lifelong student of metaphysics and spirituality, I had never been interested in crystals. Having passed through a childhood stint of devotion to Christianity, I eventually rejected the unquestioning "for-the-Bible-tells-me-so" dogma of the religion. The crystal books I had read had this same matter-of-fact tone, with firm declarations of the crystals' metaphysical properties. I wondered: How did these people get their information about the crystals? How did I know they weren't just making this information up? How would I be able to tell if all the people writing about the crystals were sincere about their work and truly devoted to helping human-kind? What if they just thought they knew a lot about crystals? Or even worse—were outright charlatans?

So I avoided crystals.

There eventually came a time when I wanted to pick out a special piece of jewelry for myself, and I aimed to find something that was energetically supportive. But I found myself disappointed with what was available. Much of the metaphys-ical jewelry I saw was poorly made and though I believed there was merit to the healing powers of crystals, I was dubious of the claims that came with the jewelry. The metaphysical properties in the descriptions of the crystals seemed to be copied from somewhere else, making the jewelry feel as if it had been created in blind faith, rather than with true understanding of the healing energy it possessed. Though I wasn't clear exactly what I was responding to, I knew that I could at least pick out stones that agreed energetically with me. So I decided to make some jewelry for myself.

I found a few stones and made myself some pieces I was happy with. But the response I got from others, how the pieces seemed to inspire and touch them, made me realize how much I would love to make healing jewelry for them too. Though I trusted my intuition to pick out stones for myself, I wasn't sure I would be able to choose the right stones for someone else. I knew I wasn't going to be comfortable making jewelry based on metaphysical descriptions I found in crystal books, so in order to feel confident standing behind my work, I needed a personal understanding of what the stones could do. I figured the best way to do this was to establish a direct relationship with the crystals and see if I could develop even an iota of intuitive understanding of the crystals myself. So I took a class in crystal healing.

It was during this course that I was assigned to facilitate a crystal healing. My teacher's friend lay on a mat as I intuitively placed crystals on her body while my teacher sat nearby to guide me in case I got stuck. But right after the session, my teacher looked at her friend, gestured to me, and said, "Can you believe this is her first time?" Facilitating the session had been quite engrossing and I was still processing the experience for myself, so I didn't exactly realize I was being complimented when I brushed the comment off, saying that it had all just made sense to me. But driving home from the class, it dawned on me: *I understood the crystals!*

I went home in a daze. All my life I had struggled, begged, and pleaded to understand what my purpose was, and suddenly, by what felt like happenstance, I was tuned in and connected to the crystals. Instead of directly telling me what my purpose was, the Universe had sent me on what had felt like a wild goose chase. All my life I had had interests in so many subjects, and I had always felt encouraged by the Universe to explore them. Sometimes I would pick up a hobby for a short while before circumstances in life forced me to change direction. Though I was intrigued with everything I learned, I found it confusing that none of the things the Universe had led me to try had any relationship to one another. I had followed each sign hoping it would lead me to my purpose, but more often than not, each situation I found myself in would feel more perilous. It felt as if the Universe was sending me deeper into the wilderness and at every fork encouraging me to take the scarier and more treacherous route. And following each nudge meant choosing the path of less stability, the path that presented an even greater chance of dire consequence if things did not turn out well.

But after many decades of what seemed like aimless wandering, traversing through what felt like bramble and bush, leading to what seemed like the edge of the world, it felt like the Universe had suddenly dropped my purpose squarely into my arms. Driving home from my crystal class, I completely understood why my life had been filled with these odd, random assignments, why I had so many disparate interests, and why I had such a seemingly disjointed career. Because on that drive I realized that everything I had ever experienced, everything I had ever learned, had turned out to be the exact training I needed in order to become a crystal healer. The Universe had had a plan all along.

———————————

I share with you this story because I have a hunch that it's your story too. You too have been searching for something, something that has always been inside of you, pulling at you, urging you to keep looking. And despite all the obstacles, the seemingly wrong turns and dead ends, you are still trying to find the answer to what you are seeking. In your life's journey, you've tried so many things in an effort to understand what you have been yearning for. You've read books, taken courses, and explored many different paths hoping it would lead you to your answer. Each time you pursued a new perspective, you learned more about who you were. And though you were able to discover new things about yourself, you still felt as if there was something more you needed to know.

You too have been on a meandering path filled with uncertainty. You too have been wandering in your search, feeling aimless at times, journeying through precarious situations, wondering if you have made the right decisions. And I want you to know, you have—because you have always been searching for your truth.

Now at this part of your journey, you have reached a place where you desire to learn more about the crystals. You have felt them pull at you, intriguing you with powers that you know are there. Somewhere inside of you is a hope that the crystals may lead you to the answers you seek—and they will, though it may be only part of the journey you are to take. But what a fun journey it will be, and what a blessing to discover that your crystals are your companions, cheering you on, supporting you, and helping you as you meet your destiny.

What I learned in that crystal course, and what I am teaching you in this book, is that connecting to crystals is all about learning to tune in to their frequencies. As you develop your intuitive skills, these frequencies will become louder and bolder as your ability to hear and feel them becomes more acute. This process will then help you develop an understanding of how to use the crystals' supportive frequencies to heal yourself as they accompany you on your ongoing journey to your truth. Many of you will discover that you actually have a deep connection to the crystals and, as in my story, will find that you know more about them than you have ever realized. But even if you find that working with crystalline energy isn't your strongest intuitive talent, upon finishing this book you will end up knowing far more about the crystals than you ever have before. Not only will your intuitive abilities be strengthened on the whole, but your perspective on crystals will be forever changed so that you will never be able to look at them in the same way again. You will be connected enough with their energies that you will be able to work with them in an intensely support-ive way and know how to get their help when you need it.

So, let us begin our journey together with the crystals.

"The great arises out of small things
that are honored and cared for."
–Eckhart Tolle, *A New Earth*

Opal in matrix

INTRODUCTION

Do you want to learn how to work with crystals?
If your answer is *yes*, this book was written for you.

I HAVE MET SO MANY OF YOU who sincerely want to learn about the crystals. Through your many questions, comments, and concerns, I profoundly hear your longing to understand crystalline energy.

In your desire to understand them, you may have gathered information here and there, hoping that all that you learned would click together and make sense in a deeper way. You found information telling you about the properties of different crystals but scant information on how to actually work with them. What you did find was in bits and pieces and often confusing and contradictory to you.

You couldn't shake the feeling there was so much more to understand.

Because you intuitively felt the gap between the power you sensed in the crystals and what you understood about them, you came to the conclusion that being in tune with the crystals—being able to understand them, communicate with them, and use them for healing—was only for a select, special few.

This is untrue.

There is a real reason why **you** are drawn to them.

You have the ability to understand and work with crystals too.

Your understanding of crystals will be forever changed by this book.

Learning about crystals is exactly like learning how to cook. First, you have to get to know your ingredients. Then, you discover techniques for how to cook with them. The more you cook, the more you learn. Over time, you begin to get a feel for what's too much, what's too little, and what's just right. And as you gain experience and skill, you no longer have to depend on the recipes someone else has written. Instead, you are able to develop new dishes based on ingredients and techniques that resonate with you and create new flavor combinations imbued with your own tastes and unique take on the world.

In the same way, you can think of this book as being like a cooking class, but one that teaches you how to "cook" with crystals. You will learn about them, understand how they work, and discover basic techniques to get you started. Then, with practice and experience, you can take these foundational methods and apply them toward more advanced forms of crystal healing. You will learn how to work with the crystals so that you may use their powerful energies to help heal yourself in all areas of your life.

HOW TO APPROACH THIS BOOK

This book is based on my experience working with crystals as a crystal healer as well as what I have found most helpful in teaching others how to use crystalline energy. For those of you just beginning your journey with crystals, this book will be an in-depth study of the basics of crystals. If you already have a connection and practice with the crystals, you are likely to discover new perspectives and approaches to working with them.

This book is different from other crystal books you might have read. Instead of focusing on individual crystals and their properties, I will be teaching you how to work with crystals in a way that gives you a direct, personal experience of their energies. In order to help you do this, I encourage you to connect with the crystals in a firsthand way by simply looking at them in the photographs and noting your reactions toward each of them before reading the captions. Additional information about the crystals in these photographs, including the size and locality of mineral specimens, appears in the Photo Information section in the back of the book. **It's also important that the chapters be read in order,** for they have been calibrated to layer the information in such a way as to maximize what you learn. Because of this, it is very important to not jump around from section to section. As you read, you will come across information that will spark related questions, and you will be tempted to skip ahead to another chapter to get your answer. But I urge you to be patient: As the old adage goes, the whole is more than the sum of its parts; and this book has been arranged in such a way that once you've completed all of the chapters and exercises in order, you will gain a far more holistic and rewarding understanding of crystalline energy.

This book has been written for someone who has a general idea of spiritual concepts like chakras, vibrations, and energy healing. But even if you don't know what these things are, don't worry, keep reading along. Even if you read a thousand poems about falling in love, you won't truly understand what everyone is making a fuss about until you experience the feeling for yourself. In the same way, true understanding of metaphysical principles comes only with personal experience, and until then the words can only serve as an outline to give you an idea of what you are seeking. But this book has been structured in such a way that you will begin to gain experience with these concepts as you work through it.

Also, by the nature of its multidimensionality, metaphysical information has to be "folded" when put into words, creating a layered quality to the text that reveals more insight over time. So it's entirely common to read a passage from a metaphysical text, then return to it at a later date and pick up entirely new information, as though you had never read the words before. Thus, metaphysical information can be much like a very intricate connect-the-dots illustration: At first you may see only a patchy outline, but the more personal experience and understanding of each metaphysical concept you gain, the more detailed and rich your picture will become. And because each picture can only continue to gain more definition, wherever you are is as good a starting place to be as any. So don't worry about what doesn't make sense now. Over time you'll understand these concepts better.

Thus, be gentle with yourself and allow yourself to have fun learning about the crystals. As long as you put sincere effort into the exercises and do your best to understand the information that follows, you can expect not only to connect to your own latent crystal abilities but to deepen your intuitive talents on the whole.

Azurites exhibiting
different crystal habits

Honoring Your Truth

As you read this book, you may find that what you have learned from other crystal teachers resonates with you more. Because the study of crystals is not a religion and, like most subjects, has different schools of thought, there are ultimately no specific rules or codified guidelines to follow. Because every teacher will have a different opinion, it will be up to you to decide what information best connects with your spiritual energies (though you'll always know you're on the right path if what you learn and practice makes you truly *feel* better).

Thus it is very important to trust your own experience rather than believe what someone else says. This includes anything I write about the crystals. If you disagree with something in this book, that's okay. Give yourself permission to have a different opinion about part or all of what you learn. This book will hone your intuition and your intuition with crystals, so ultimately it is far more important to trust your own experience than to believe someone else's truth, including mine.

HOW TO PREPARE FOR THE EXERCISES IN THIS BOOK

YOU WILL NEED THREE SMALL CRYSTALS to do the exercises in this book. Though you have until the end of chapter 9 to get the crystals, I strongly suggest doing this step first, for once you begin to connect to your intuition, you won't want anything keeping you from doing these exercises.

Crystals in the size you need are typically called "tumbled stones" or "pocket stones" and range in price from very inexpensive to very expensive, depending on their rarity. But how much they cost doesn't matter. **What matters is keeping the identity of these crystals secret for the exercises.** This means sending someone else to pick up the stones for you. Alternatively, you can purchase a premade kit of concealed crystals especially created for the exercises in this book from my online crystal shop at place8healing.com.

If a friend is picking the stones for you, have them visit a metaphysical or crystal shop in person or online and buy three pocket-size stones. They do not need to know what stones you already own, as it does not matter for this exercise. Twenty dollars should be sufficient to purchase a set of pocket stones.

INSTRUCTIONS FOR YOUR FRIEND:

1   Purchase three different pocket stones from the list on the next page.

2   Designate each crystal as "A," "B," or "C," and on a piece of paper write a key that lists the letters and corresponding names of the stones.

3   Conceal the crystals by separately wrapping each stone in a blank sheet of paper. Try to wrap all packages thickly and make them about the same size (you want to do your best to conceal the shapes of the crystals). Then clearly mark each package with its matching designated letter. Securely tape the packages closed.

4   Seal the key in an opaque envelope.

5   Give your friend the envelope along with the three packages.

STONES TO CHOOSE FROM: The following is a suggested list of stones that have been selected for their wide availability. If possible, choose stones from this list.

- Amazonite
- Amethyst
- Angelite (aka blue anhydrite)
- Aquamarine
- Black tourmaline
- Blue lace agate
- Green aventurine
- Hematite
- Kyanite (blue colored)
- Lepidolite
- Malachite
- Mangano/manganoan calcite
- Moonstone

- Obsidian (black or mostly black colored)
- Prehnite
- Pyrite
- Red jasper
- Rhodochrosite
- Rhodonite
- Rose quartz
- Selenite
- Smoky quartz
- Sodalite
- Tiger's eye

ONCE YOU HAVE THE STONES: **Don't squeeze the packages to feel the shape of the stones!** The less you know about the stones, the better your results will be. So keep it a surprise! Save the stones for exercise 5, following chapter 9.

Calcite concretion (aka Fairy Stone)

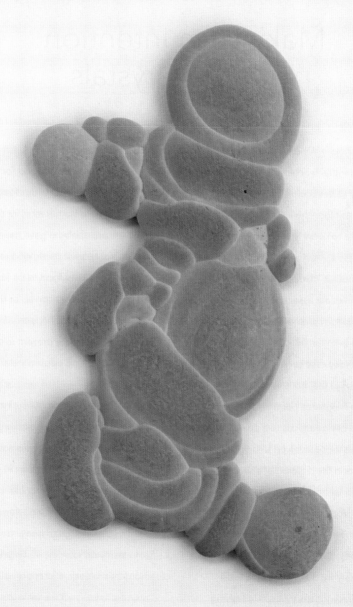

"This above all:
to thine own self be true."
—William Shakespeare, *Hamlet*

with your "favorite movies" across from a "comfy couch" with a "purring cat." It may not be your prototypical idea of a cozy room and in fact may be entirely different than anything you would think of, but the room, with its feeling of intimacy, comfort, relaxation, and safety, would fit perfectly within your *feeling* of a "cozy room." Thus, the *feeling* of a cozy room better encapsulates the idea and expands the range of what is possible than any physical list of attributes you could think up. So returning to our exercise, focusing on the *feeling* prevents you from having a vision that is too specific, while both summarizing and encompassing the totality of your intention without eliminating other potential outcomes that would make you equally satisfied.

The feelings you choose then act as signals to let you know you have moved toward your intention. As you progress and get closer to it, you will *feel* different than when you began. And as you continue, this feeling will deepen, becoming more prominent and clear to you.

Though you may have aimed to get a specific result, it's important to recognize that your intention will have an open-ended quality and no true, clear goal to reach. Instead your intention acts as a focus for you to move toward in your ongoing journey.

Following are the steps to take for your intention ceremony. Read through them to familiarize yourself with the process, then sit down, close your eyes, and follow the ceremony as best as you can remember. This ceremony is less about precision and more about being as present and clear as you can in this specific space and time with your intent.

1. Find a quiet place to sit down. Sit either cross-legged on the floor or in a chair with your feet on the ground.

2. Close your eyes and take three deep breaths. Make these breaths slow, long, and as deep as possible.

3. Turn your attention inward toward your body. Imagine your head and spine glowing softly with a golden light. Then expand this glow to a bubble of golden light that generously surrounds your entire body.

4. Once you have a firm vision or sensation of your golden bubble, think of your intention and its feeling. Imagine holding this feeling in your heart.

5. Once you have the intention's energy held in your heart, call upon any of your spirit guides, crystal guides, angels, and any additional teachers of light to be with you. Ask them for their help and support in your journey in understanding the crystals.

6. Take three more slow, deep breaths, and then gently open your eyes.

Congratulations on completing your first exercise!

Crystal Healing Is
the Deepest Healing

The type of crystal healing I practice takes clients on an encompassing inner journey. Lying down, the client closes their eyes, and as I place crystals on their body they begin to see visions.

At first they may only see faint colors and shapes, but soon enough they see distinct images and find themselves in landscapes that they experience in a surprisingly visceral way. As they explore their surroundings the client and I have a back and forth, as if we are having an ordinary conversation, except that the client is also immersed in an interior world, interacting with the beings and objects within it.

My job is to hold space; that is, to create an environment both physical and energetic that keeps the client safe and protected while encouraging any energies needing to be healed to play out and be processed. This means I must be fully present, my energy tethered and grounded, and my total attention focused on facilitating the client's journey. I monitor the client's energies as they shift and change while also intuitively keeping tabs on what is happening within their visions. I ask them questions to help them along.

"Where are you?"

"I'm in a forest."

"What do you see?"

"I see a cave."

"Would you like to go in the cave?"

"No!" they emphatically reply.

"Why?"

"Because it's dark."

"Hold on—" I say, rearranging some crystals and placing a new one on them. *"What do you see now?"*

"I can see inside the cave."

"What do you see in the cave?"

"I see a fur bed, a warm fire, and paintings on the wall."

"Would you like to go in now?"

"Yes."

And so they enter the cave to discover the information waiting inside for them.

My job is also to function as a kind of tour guide to the client's inner worlds. Though exactly what kind of world the client will enter is always a surprise, I do know how to navigate these alternate realities. Since the environments and people they encounter can be quite unusual, clients are often perplexed by situations they find themselves in. But because I hold the space, I can be both "outside" of their experience and have a bird's-eye view of what is happening to them within it. This allows me to have a wider perspective on what the client is experiencing as well as an understanding of the significance of what they are going through. This enables me to ask the kind of questions that help the client make better sense of what is happening to them. Though ultimately it is the client's choice to decide where they will go and how they will proceed in their visions, as an experienced tour guide I can make the most intriguing suggestions on where they may go to reach the kind of healing they are yearning for.

While the client is having adventures in their inner worlds, I sit by them, adding, removing, and shifting crystals on and around their body depending on what is happening with their energies. I often say my experience of facilitating a crystal healing session feels akin to that of an audio engineer on a sound board adjusting levels (*"More bass! Less treble! Less reverb all around!"*). But instead of calibrating with switches, sliders, and knobs, I help calibrate the energies of the client by using the energetic patterns produced by a variety of crystals. Depending on the kinds of adjustments a person needs, I can use the crystals to give a lift to any energies that could use a boost, realign energies that have become skewed, and/or coax out any supportive energies that may have been previously submerged.

When the inner part of their journey is completed and it's time for the client to open their eyes, I hand them a mirror so that they can see themselves and the crystals that have been laid on their body. Upon seeing their reflection, with perhaps the hundred or so crystals on and around themselves, they often remark that they had no idea so many had been used. Having been so deep in their inner journey, they never even felt the crystals being placed upon their skin.

The interior worlds experienced in a crystal healing session have a dreamlike quality. Situations and environments morph and change in a fluid way and are seen from a perspective that feels far more aware and expanded than anything experienced in ordinary life. But although the visions have an ephemeral quality to them, the experience itself is profoundly visceral. In addition to feeling definite sensations in their body, a person is able to hear, taste, and smell objects in their inner environment. Emotions are profoundly felt because of how intensely and clearly they are experienced. A client will find themselves speaking with people who have personalities distinct from their own, while also discovering they are able to telepathically communicate with objects and animals. Sometimes they have conversations with loved ones no longer physically present or with children yet to be born. Sometimes they recall what they had believed to be an insignificant memory, only to discover that their experience had a far deeper impact on their life than they previously realized. They may even recall an event that as an adult they fully understand but may find the child who initially experienced it still within themselves, in deep hurt and pain. And sometimes clients travel even further back, into their past lives, discovering ancient traumas that continue to affect them in their current lives. In these ways and more, crystal healing allows unfinished energetic pieces to be surfaced, attended to, processed, and healed. And each healed piece becomes significant in understanding and resolving the challenges the person has been experiencing within their present life.

This occurs because crystal healing, like other kinds of energy work, affects the *subtle bodies*. Although you have likely spent your whole life identifying yourself by what you have seen in the mirror, this is not all of who you are. What you have seen is a reflection of your physical body, but you are far more than just that.

Perhaps you believe your identity also consists of a thing you have called a soul, but this is a bit of a misnomer as well. This is because your soul is not something you *possess*;

"If you want to find the secrets
of the Universe, think in terms of
energy, frequency, and vibration."
—Nikola Tesla

Smoky Quartz

your soul is the most essential part of who you are. You *are* a soul that *has* a body, not the other way around! Your soul is not something you *have*. Instead, it is actually your physical body that you "borrow" and "have" for this lifetime, while your soul can exist independently outside of your physical form.

But you have other "bodies" that make up who are you are as well. There are many different ways to categorize them, but generally speaking, you have four major bodies— the *physical*, *emotional*, *mental*, and *spiritual*. While the *physical* body is what you see in the mirror and your *spiritual* body is your soul, your *mental* and *emotional* bodies are additional nonphysical portions of your being. Together, your nonphysical bodies (the mental, emotional, and spiritual) are collectively known as your *subtle bodies*.

Unlike your physical body, which has a density that is material, your subtle bodies are so much lighter, finer, and more "subtle" in form that they cannot be perceived by any physical means. Just like your physical body, each one of your subtle bodies is contained in a contiguous form. Emerging from deep within you and expanding past your body, the subtle bodies surround you in layers of increasingly lighter energy. While your physical body is your densest, most material layer, surrounding it is a layer of lighter energy known as your emotional body. Extending past the emotional body is your mental body, whose energy has even lesser density than that of the emotional body. But it is your spiritual body (aka your soul) that has the lightest and most encompassing energy of all. Not only does your spiritual body surround all your layers, sheathing and holding them, it also emerges from the deepest and most core part of who you are. It is your spiritual body that is most essential to your being.

Combined, your subtle bodies make up what is known as your *aura*, a field of energy that radiates beyond your physical self. While your physical body has been adapted to interact with the physical dimension, your aura exists beyond the constraints of fixed space and time. But although your aura is multidimensional, you still experience your subtle bodies all the time in the physical dimension. This is because your subtle bodies, along with your physical body, each govern a different part of you, distinguishing themselves by communicating to you with their own particular "point of view." This is why you are able to have wildly disparate reactions to the same circumstance, all at the same time.

For example, perhaps something happens to you that makes you want to cry. Though the feelings are welling up inside of you, you hold back the tears because you believe it's an inappropriate time to cry, yet your eyes start to glisten and the tears begin falling from your eyes. In this case, your emotional, mental, and physical bodies each have their own particular way of responding to the same situation. Meanwhile, your spiritual body, whose aim is to gain experience and wisdom, has a more neutral approach to the dramas of daily life.

While the rest of your bodies do all the conversing, debating, negotiating, and comparing with each other, the spiritual body steps back and takes a role more akin to that of an observer. For out of all the bodies, the spiritual body is the most connected to the truest understanding of timelessness, so it is in no rush to resolve any imbalances it experiences. Instead, knowing that you are already destined to move toward enlightenment, it allows any experience you go through to fully play out.

But what your spiritual body *does* do is consistently impel you toward an even greater state of balance and truth by quietly beckoning you in a deep and steady way. This is why, despite any protests or disagreements from any of your other bodies (like "logical" arguments prepared by your mind or emotional fears of abject failure), you can still always *feel* something pulling at you, calling you, constantly letting you know, like a cosmic game of Marco Polo, that there is more to know—and more to yourself—than you have settled for. And because the journey of the soul is everlasting, no matter what truths about yourself you uncover, there will always be another, even deeper part of your soul still to be found.

Where the issue comes in is when a schism develops between the different "departments." As in the example above, the feelings of wanting to cry (emotional body) and the action of actually crying (physical body) are congruent with the desire of the spiritual body, which is to honor your truth and cry. Your body is on board, your emotions are on board, your spirit is on board, but your mind (mental body) has decided that this is a highly improper circumstance to display your emotions. The mind then tries any number of methods to overwhelm the other departments in order to take control of the situation. Perhaps it pulls out a rulebook of social behavior, stating that crying in public is only for the weak, and overpowers the emotional body into feeling shame. Then the physical body responds, stopping the tears by making the teeth grit, the eyes harden, and the body tense. So the flow of emotional and physical energy that would have come to completion had you cried and honestly expressed yourself instead becomes bottled up inside of you.

If this energy does not get released, it begins to fester. But first, it looks for some sort of place it can reside. Like a pest, it searches for any suitable nook or cranny in one or more of your bodies that it can squeeze into and inhabit. Perhaps it wants to wedge itself into the mind, blending into the multitude of other social anxieties that have previously found their way in. Maybe it finds itself nestling into the emotional body, cloaking itself not as pain but as misdirected anger. Or perhaps this repressed energy finds its way into the physical body, adding just a bit more tension to the muscles of the heart. Until this energy is released it becomes stuck somewhere inside of you, and the longer it stays in your body the more aggravated it becomes. And because this energy has now found a way to take up residence inside you, like a magnet it attracts other energies just like it to join in and squat together.

At first, the pain may be vaguely noticeable, or perhaps not noticeable at all. But as time goes on the unreleased energy begins to ulcerate, and as this energy continues to churn upon itself the sensation of pain increases. Whether the pain is emotional, mental, or physical, your bodies are trying to tell you that something is very wrong. And that is simply what pain is: a signal to let you know something is not right.

No matter which body it expresses itself in, every iota of pain and imbalance is also registered in your spiritual body. This is because your spiritual body encompasses the other bodily layers. Overseeing all "departments," it reflects any of the incongruencies happening anywhere within it. But while feeling soul pain is distressing, it comes with a great benefit. Because your spiritual body holds all the other bodily layers, it is in direct connection with each one of them at the same time, so any pain found in any layer can be influenced to heal through healing of the spiritual body.

This is how you can be healed with energy. Because the spiritual body is a subtle body, it can be affected by other subtle energies, including the energies produced by crystals. Via the aura, the spiritual body is able to interact with crystalline energies in the same parallel, nonphysical, multidimensional frequency. Then imbalances that are resolved in the spiritual body can be reflected in the layer of the body that originated them. But healing imbalances on one bodily layer also creates a cascade of other beneficial effects because of the way your spiritual body is interconnected with all other layers. So as in the previous example, if one uses a modality like crystal healing to heal pain in the mental body (letting the mind know it's okay to cry), it can in turn release constrictions in the emotional body (allowing the most honest feelings to come forth), which then releases tension from the physical body (letting the body shed tears). This series of changes shifts the various bodies into a truer and more honest state, which consequently influences the spiritual body on the whole by allowing it to be in a greater state of balance with itself. Resonating more deeply with its own truth, the soul's energy becomes clearer and more radiant, and this energy becomes outwardly expressed as greater happiness and fulfillment in one's life.

This is why crystal healing and other modalities aimed at healing at the soul level are so incredibly powerful. For instead of working on separate layers one at a time, modalities like this follow the threads of energy that connect all the way to your true core—your soul—to heal you at the very deepest level of your being. And though the type of crystal healing sessions I facilitate is meant to be especially intense and cathartic, you can still get all the soul-healing benefits of crystals working with them on your own. All you need to do is to learn to work with them in sincerity, integrity, and love, and they will show you how to deeply heal your soul.

CHAPTER 1

WHY CRYSTALS ARE IMPORTANT

IN PAST LIVES, you have worked with crystals and stones as tools of healing, at a time when the power of these mineral beings was accepted and commonplace. Because of this, you came into this life with the persistent hunch that crystals are more than inanimate objects dug out of the earth. You have a vague sense there's something more. This is why you are so compelled by them.

But there's a reason why you don't remember much of the information.

You have had hundreds, or more likely thousands, of past lives. If you were able to recall the details from all these lifetimes, you would be overwhelmed. Every day you would find yourself dwelling on the memories of love and loss from millions of past relationships. The sheer volume of information you would remember would be so preoccupying that you wouldn't have any mental space to spare for your present life. All your fears would carry over, and your life would be filled with constant anxiety and dread.

Thus, in order to function in your present life, you are given a fresh start with a seemingly blank memory to allow you to explore and play in the dynamics of your life without being bogged down by constant flashbacks. Though your past life history stays permanently recorded, memories from these lifetimes remain cloaked so that you may have the mental and emotional space to maximize the lessons you have come to learn now in your current life.

But your past lives bleed through. You may have an unexplained interest in a specific historical time period or a passion for a subject unrelated to the environment you grew up in. Civil War reenactors, Renaissance fair enthusiasts, and even a doctor from Japan fanatical about American bluegrass music—all point to past lives influencing a current life. You also bring talents, big and small, from past lives. A person may have a gift for an unusual sport when no one else in their family has any athletic ability. An artistically gifted child can be born into a family with absolutely no history or interest in art. You may visit a foreign city for the first time and somehow immediately know your way around. You may not remember specific memories but may find that you have a connection to and knowledge about things you have had no prior experience with in this lifetime. And there are other ways your past lives will echo into your current life. You can meet someone for the first time and immediately and profoundly like (or dislike) them before even knowing their name because of a relationship you had with them in a past life.

And so too it is with your past lives with crystals. Though you don't remember the specifics, you know there is something special about them. You have a sense they are powerful, but you don't know how or why. You find yourself continuing to collect them, even when you're not sure what to do with them. This is all because of your past lives working with crystals. Your memories with them are shrouded, but your interest in them follows you into this lifetime.

CRYSTALS ARE PART OF YOUR SOUL'S HISTORY

The greatest period in our crystal history was during the time of Atlantis. This ancient civilization intimately understood the power of crystalline energy and used crystals as a key form of technology to power their culture. Much as petroleum is used to generate energy for our modern world, crystals and other subtle energy technologies were used to generate energy in their world. Knowledge of crystals was widespread and commonplace among all of humanity because of the influence of this powerful ancient civilization.

But as time went on, Atlanteans began using crystalline technology with darker motives. As many crystals are inherently neutral and can be manipulated to produce negative energy, people began using crystals to feed their growing materialism, greed, and power, steering the crystalline energy to manipulate and control people instead of benefiting humanity. It reached a point where Atlantean society became so corrupted that in order to save humanity the Universe had to put a dramatic halt to its misguided trajectory.

You are most likely familiar with the biblical story of Noah and the great flood. But the Hebrews weren't the only ones with a flood story: The Dogon of Africa, the Norse, the ancient Egyptians, the Inuit, the Greek, the ancient Chinese, the Sumerians, and the Aborigines are among the nearly two thousand other cultures that tell of a great flood that came and decimated the world. With a giant sweep of water the planet flooded and the Universe buried, among other knowledge, the accumulated encyclopedia of crystal understanding. The few who survived the tragedy lost everything. Lacking the collective information to re-create the technologies that had made the Atlantean civilization so great, the survivors were thrust back into a primitive existence. All they had left to share with the generations they bore after them were fantastical stories of an almighty culture that had once existed before the terrible flood came to wash them back into the Dark Ages.

You may have been one of those who misused crystals during this time. But fortunately, you have had many lives since then to resolve your past karma. In facing the consequences of misusing crystals, you had many experiences of struggle and pain, but through all these hard knocks, you learned many lessons of love and compassion. During these lifetimes of learning and healing, you were purposely distanced from your soul's own crystalline knowledge because you were not yet ready to work with its power in a disciplined and loving way.

But humanity's energy has been evolving and growing. Over time, we have moved farther away from our fearful tribal pasts to a more understanding and holistic global worldview. Overall, humanity has become more spiritually evolved. We've become more inclusive not only of other human beings but also of animals, plants, and the Earth we live upon. There are still plenty of people playing out their last desperate vestiges of greed and selfishness, but there are a great many of us, many more than ever before, who have been opening to the light of consciousness and are holding space for healing energies to be here on Earth. As our hearts have become more evolved and as we collectively become a more compassionate species, we, now more than ever, are becoming responsible enough to hold and use the healing energies of the crystals for the benefit of our planet. This is why you have been finding yourself increasingly drawn to crystals. It means you too have a role to play in helping to heal our world.

CRYSTAL GRIDS HEAL THE WORLD

Since the cataclysmic flood that submerged Atlantis, the world has significantly changed. Human civilization has become increasingly global. You can easily fly to a country halfway across the world or instantly share information with remote parts of the globe through the magic of the internet. As intellectual information increasingly moves from place to place, intellectual energy moves with it and connects humans in the modern world with one another.

Also being moved is crystalline energy.

Not only do crystals hold healing vibrations associated with the kinds of minerals they are, but they also hold an energetic resonance connected to the specific place that gave birth to them. With the global economy, a mineral that was once isolated to one part of the world can now be moved to a new location along with its unique metaphysical energies. As people awaken to the crystals, find themselves drawn to them, and begin collecting and taking care of them, they help facilitate the energies being produced by the crystals. And whether they are aware of it or not, people who truly love crystals have become participants in elevating the energies of the world.

This is because people who collect crystals are inadvertently creating crystal grids. Each crystal has a different energy, which can be combined with those of other crystals to coordinate their healing energies. Like different musical notes played together to create a harmonic chord, combinations of crystals can also be created to produce an energetic synergy, or "grid" of energy. Harmonics created by a crystal grid can act as an energetic "key" unlocking previously closed portals of energy and causing them to open.

Energetic portals are located all over Mother Earth, and as more people acquire crystals and learn to work with them they are both consciously and unconsciously activating crystal portals around where they live. As these portals open, the energy of light and consciousness is able to come through from the subtle spiritual realms to be grounded in the physical world. The combined opening and activating of these portals allows the giant crystalline grid energetically surrounding the whole Earth to increase in its ability to hold spiritual light, which then lifts the energy of the entire world!

When we speak of elevating our energies or the energies of the Earth, we are talking about resonating in a higher frequency. The higher the frequency, the more evolved the energy is and the closer/deeper it is to universal divine energy. Since spiritual growth is an ongoing process into infinity, there is no actual final destination and no ultimate frequency to attain. Rather, your goal is to constantly raise this frequency.

Anything that moves you toward love and compassion will raise your frequency. Thus things like violence and hatred are low frequency, while things like benevolence and humility are high frequency. Spiritual healing includes anything that heals one's pain and suffering, whether in this current life or in lives past. Therefore any spiritual healing will bring you closer to love, thus raising your frequency.

Crystals are one of the many modalities that raise one's frequency by helping to bring healing and elevate one's energies. And as everyone is connected to one another, raising one's own individual frequency helps to raise the collective frequency of the world.

THE TIPPING POINT

Every thought you have creates a vibrational resonance. Every idea or concept has a vibrational resonance too. As people begin thinking, talking, or working through an idea, it causes that specific vibrational resonance to magnify. At first, this resonance is perceived only by a few. But over time, as more people think about the same thing, the specific vibrational resonance increases, like the volume knob of a stereo being turned up. As more and more people join in, the intensity of this resonance becomes exponential. Suddenly it hits a critical mass and the idea ripples out to the rest of the collective.

This is what is happening with crystals. The collective vibration of many people thinking, talking, and working with crystals is suddenly infiltrating the collective consciousness of humanity. As human beings we have been putting a significant amount of energy into heart-centered healing. We are far more accepting and compassionate of other human beings who are different from us than we have ever been in our history's past. Now that we can easily communicate and hear firsthand stories from our brothers and sisters all over the world, we are better able to understand their lives without being hindered by the racism, sexism, and the classism of the past. And despite all the madness in the world, we have made incredible progress opening our hearts. As our hearts become more open, our ability to be compassionate and kind increases, allowing love, the highest vibration in the Universe, to manifest through us. And now, because so many of us are generating, practicing, and contributing to this high vibration, the crystals, already emanating a high vibration, are harmonically able to work with us again, to assist us in healing ourselves and the whole world.

OPPOSITE: Quartz egg with rutile and   ABOVE: Pyrite with quartz
other unknown inclusions

Popular Misconceptions about Crystals

Because crystals are so effective at healing, they get an exalted status as metaphysical tools. But the way crystals are popularly presented oversimplifies them into a kind of metaphysical "drug." One is "prescribed" a crystal for whatever symptom ails them, and the healing effects of each stone are turned into petty generalizations of material outcome. (*"Want to attract a romantic relationship? Try this stone! Want to make more money? Try that stone! Want to lose weight? Try some other stone!"*)

Not only does this kind of information lead to the misinterpretation of a crystal's benefits, it also leads to a misunderstanding of how crystals work. The overwhelming focus on crystals for their specific metaphysical properties demeans crystals and shrouds their true powers in a convenient "quick-fix" package. This causes crystals to be treated like the kinds of objects that are used then disposed of without afterthought once they no longer seem useful. For this reason, much of the popularly disseminated, overly facile information about crystals and their metaphysical properties is detrimental both to the person seeking crystal healing and to the crystal itself.

This is not to say that metaphysical descriptions of crystals are completely unuseful, for they can be helpful in orienting yourself to a crystal's general purpose. But like two different people playing the same instrument, the interaction of your energy with a crystal creates a unique harmonic resonance that generates a different range of specific healing effects than it would on someone else. This is one of the things most misunderstood about crystal energy and is why it's unhelpful to rely solely on a description of a crystal's metaphysical properties to determine which crystal is best for you and your situation.

The oversimplification of these properties also extends to another popular misconception about crystals. Crystals are often promoted as objects that will miraculously fix whatever problem you have just by your owning them. This is false. Simply having a crystal does not confer healing benefits. Like screwdrivers, paring knives, or paintbrushes, crystals are tools—and the results you get from them depend on how well you use them. When working with any tool, you will learn techniques and gain skill and experience that help you better use your tool to create your desired result. It's the same with crystals.

Crystals are beings with feelings, wants, and desires. They absolutely love helping people. But the process of being able to access their powerful abilities and allowing them to help you lies in connecting to the crystals in a deep and profound way. It also means understanding how they work and working in conjunction with them rather than treating them like some kind of energetic appliance that puts in all the effort of fixing your life for you.

Through this book, you will develop skills that will help you personally understand crystals in an intimate and meaningful way. By discovering and developing your intuitive abilities, you will be able to learn far more about the crystals than you would from reading about their metaphysical descriptions in some book. By empowering yourself with crystals in this way, not only will you be able to maximize the healing benefits you get, but you will also bring a much-desired honor and respect to the crystals by being able to work with them as the sentient, compassionate, and healing beings that they are.

A Warm-Up

The steps below are a simple warm-up exercise
to get you in the practice of observing.

1. Get a notepad and set a timer for ten minutes.

2. Find a window with some kind of view to look out of.

3. Start the timer and begin writing down everything you see, hear, and feel. (You can write your observations longform in a stream of consciousness, or in a bulleted list.)

4. **Be as detailed as possible with what you write down.** Especially write down the things you would think are insignificant.

How did it go? Did you feel like you wrote down a lot? If you didn't, it's okay. Again, this exercise is about getting into the practice of *observing*.

5. Now take a second pass. Read the questions opposite and repeat the exercise to see if you can be more detailed in what you observe. This time, imagine you're using the zoom on your camera. Observe the big items first and then "zoom" into the details (or vice versa).

If you happen to be looking at a tree, here are some points of observation to note:

- How small or large is the tree?

- Do you know what species of tree it is?

- Is the tree young or old?

- If the tree is green, what color green is it? If it's not green, what other color (or colors) is it?

- Describe the tree's shape. Perhaps straight and long, or shaped like a Christmas tree?

- What kind of textures does the tree have on its bark; on its leaves?

- Is wind or anything else moving the tree?

- Are there any animals, plants, or other objects in or around the tree?

Is there a particular person you are noticing? Describe this person:

- Are they young or old?

- What is their gender?

- What are they wearing? What kind of occasion are they dressed for? What do their clothes represent?

- What colors are they wearing?

- What is this person doing? What kind of movements are they making? Are they sitting? Are they walking slowly or quickly?

If you see buildings, observe:

- What kinds of buildings are you looking at (e.g., a high-rise office, a restaurant, a hospital, a modern house)?

- Are the buildings large or small? What kind of shapes do they form?

- What colors are the buildings?

- Do they remind you of any time period? In what decade or era do they seem to have been constructed?

- What are the buildings' windows like? Are there many windows? What are their shapes?

- What details do you notice on the buildings?

- Is there any movement associated with the buildings (e.g., people coming in and out or smoke rising from a chimney)?

Observe the sky:

- What color is it? Try going into more depth than just writing down a color like "blue." Is the sky a light blue or a deep blue? Is there a pink tint from the sunset?

- Do you see clouds? Describe their texture. What do the clouds look like?

- What is the weather like?

Other things to notice:

- With all colors, try to best identify what specific color you see. If something is red, is it cherry red, burgundy red, rust red, or some other hue? Is something navy blue, baby blue, aqua, cobalt, or another color?

- Are there any sounds coming from the environment? Traffic outside, a plane going by, people talking, a dog barking?

- What is the movement you're noticing most? Is it the clouds drifting by, people walking, birds flying?

- Are there any signs you notice: street signs, signs on buildings, billboards?

Here is an example from someone who has done the exercise:

I see a street with two-way traffic. I hear the sounds of vehicles as they approach, pass, and move in the distance. I especially notice the sound of air brakes on trucks. The traffic light alternates between bright red and green.

There are trees lining the sidewalk on both sides. Their foliage is full and deep green and they are old enough to crack the sidewalks in many places with their multiple roots. I see a self-parking sign in red and white. I see many muted gray parking meters with parked cars. The cars are mostly small and compact. A small white purse dog is on a leash with an older woman in medium-blue denim capris and tennis shoes.

The sky is hazy and colored in a combination of blue and gray. I see many redbrick buildings the color of terra-cotta clay. One awning has its name written in white. The apartment building has a sign that is mostly in red and black. But white is always found in all the signs. Both the signs and the buildings are rectangular or square.

I see a bistro. There are multiple small circular tables. The tables are brown on top with gold on the edge. The legs of the tables are ornate. The chairs are thatched and woven.

There is a soft breeze. A wide variety of people are walking by. I notice their age, race, gender, and clothing are all different. I can hear them speak in multiple languages and accents. A small black-and-white dog on a leash is being walked by their owner in a bright red-print dress. Upon closer observation, I notice the dog is a terrier mix. The dog is middle-aged and calm.

Keep your list of observations.
You will be reviewing them again later.

Sand Dune Jasper

CHAPTER 2

HOW CRYSTAL HEALING WORKS

IMAGINE HOLDING TWO TUNING FORKS of the exact same pitch. Striking one fork will make it sound—but the untouched fork will begin to vibrate and ring too. In physics this is known as sympathetic resonance: when a passive object responds to external vibrations that are harmonically alike. The same principle is at work when an opera singer breaks a champagne glass using her voice. By singing at a pitch matching the frequency of the glass, the singer causes the molecules in the glass to vibrate so powerfully they tear apart, causing the glass to shatter.

Science has proven that light, color, X-rays, and radio waves are all vibrations—even objects that are perceived to be solid are made of vibrating atoms. Since you are also made of atoms, you vibrate as well, but you can break down your vibrations into different parts. Your heart will have its own vibration. Your brain will have its own vibration. Your kidneys, spleen, and bones will have their own vibrations too. And together, your whole body will vibrate in a collective symphony that is unique to you.

However, your physical body is only part of your symphony. There are other parts of you vibrating as well. Of major influence on your overall vibration are those of your thoughts and feelings . . . and some of your thoughts and feelings may be out of whack. There could be negative thoughts running through your head or unresolved emotions from times when you had your feelings hurt. Perhaps you have gone through a traumatic event that has deeply affected your life, or you feel continued grief about something that has happened to you. Situations like these can cause notes—perhaps even whole instruments—in your symphony to go off-key. Over time you will hear your song played off-key so often that this distorted version will begin to sound normal to you. You will find ways to adjust your life to make your song workable, but you won't be able to shake the vague, nagging hunch that something isn't quite right. But because it will have been so long since you've heard your song played in tune, you will have forgotten what your song was originally supposed to sound like.

This is where the crystals can help: While you are a complex symphony of shifting vibrations, crystals have simplified energies. Each crystal emanates a single and specific vibrational tone. You can therefore use their vibrational tones to align an out-of-key vibration. As long as you open yourself up and accept working with a crystal, bringing it into your energy field allows it to act as a reference tone for your energies to align with. Your subtle bodies will be able to hear what the note was supposed to sound like and can use the crystal's vibration to retune yourself, allowing your song to be played as it was originally intended. And because the corrected vibration is more harmonized and more aligned with your true self, it results in you feeling better. Your personal symphony can then become more balanced and in tune, allowing your soul to vibrate with more clarity its deepest truth and unique beauty.

In other words, crystals act as tuning forks for your soul.

Crystals Are Tectonic

The various kinds of energy healing are like basketball, bowling, water polo, and tennis. Though they are all sports, and sports that use balls, the differences between them are vast. It's the same with energy healing.

The more well-known modalities of energy healing are usually defined by the way vibrational energy is directed: Acupuncture utilizes needles to direct energy through a body's energy meridians, Reiki uses a specific "bandwidth" of healing energy channeled through the practitioner's hands, and homeopathy uses vibrational patterns that have been transferred and embedded into a physical substance like water or sugar pills. Other modalities are nonspecific with regard to the techniques and tools used but are characterized by the specific area they target, like aura cleansing, chakra balancing, and past life therapy. Then there are modalities categorized together because of their broader similarities, like shamanism, where many different techniques are utilized depending on which cultural lineage the shaman comes from. And these examples are only a few of the hundreds of different kinds of energy healing that are available to you.

Each modality differs in the way it interacts with your energetic bodies and how you experience the healing. Some modalities will make you so relaxed that you fall asleep, while others keep you awake and alert. Some will primarily be felt as physical sensations, while others are visionary experiences that transport you to other worlds. Some modalities are gentle, soft, and soothing, while others are intense and cathartic. The combination of these varying degrees of tools, techniques, and sensory experiences results in each modality having its own distinct energetic texture. Though these healing modalities are practiced in different ways, they still aim for the same goal—to move you closer to becoming a fully healed spiritual being. Crystal healing's distinction from other modalities is that the primary tools used in the work are crystals—Mother Earth's energy contained in material form.

Crystals are often popularized as a type of energetic "pill" to treat a specific "symptom" and as some sort of attractant (or repellent) for their circumstances in life. But this oversimplified view does not allow them to be used to their full energetic potential. More often than not, the deep and intense healing energy of the crystals remains untapped because of the superficial way crystals are popularly perceived to work.

Crystals are tectonic. Because the healing energy in crystals texturally parallels the same energies used by Mother Earth to create them, using crystals is not a mild way to heal. If she wishes, Mother Earth can dramatically transform her body's landscapes through fierce movements: Pushing, pulling, subjugating, crashing, shaking, liquefying, and exploding are just some of the forces she uses to manipulate and change her body. She shifts large masses of land through the movement of her plates while compressing and melting stones with her awesome power as she sees fit. Mother Earth's energy is forceful and powerful, and this energy of hers is intrinsically placed within the crystals. Though certain crystals will have energy that is relatively gentle and soothing, on the whole, crystalline energy is intense.

The geological definition of a crystal is a solid material whose atomic components are arranged in a highly ordered and repeating pattern. This pattern is known as a *crystal lattice*. Much like a skeletal framework built with a kid's Tinkertoy construction set, it can be added upon by building both upward and outward, following the pattern begun by the foundational shape. At a certain point, you are able to see a distinct shape made of planes and faces. This cumulative structure is what we see as a crystal.

But this growing and building energy has been overemphasized in the popular understanding of crystals and their healing benefits. Most metaphysical descriptions of crystals focus on the "creating" side of crystalline energy and talk about what attributes—material, spiritual, or emotional—can be brought into and built upon a person's life. For example, you often find metaphysical descriptions that follow the formula "[Insert type of crystal here] **brings** [insert desired result]" (for example, "Citrine **brings** good luck!" or "Rose quartz **brings** true love!"). But this fixation on individual crystals only for their building energies causes people to miss how important the destructive aspect of crystalline energy is.

If you wanted to be fresh and clean, you could put on some clean clothes. But if you were caked in mud, it would be better to take a shower and wash away the grime prior to putting on a freshly washed outfit. In the same way, the popular attitude with crystals is to put energy on top of a situation rather than resolving the underlying issue first. This is why people will have mediocre results working with crystals. If the

Beryl

underlying energies are not resolved, the outcome will be self-defeating. Mother Earth uses cataclysmic energies to transform herself, so you must be willing to interact with the more ferocious aspects of crystalline energy in order to reap its full rewards. But because you are a child made from Mother Earth's body, you are already inherently able to handle all her energies, including any of her energies of destruction.

The process can be intense, but when you allow crystals to tectonically shift your energy, it clears space for new patterns of energy to thrive. The patterns that once undermined you are now recycled and transmuted into energy for building. Just as you might take a Mr. Potato Head toy with its eyes misplaced on its ass and put its parts back in the right places, the destroying and recycling energies of the crystals rearrange your parts so that your soul's flow of energy can be maximized. Your "eyes" can then be placed squarely on your face, looking forward into life, instead of upside down and behind it. The cumulative effect of repositioned energies causes a major shift in perspective. This changes how you look at everything in life, allowing you to see new avenues of opportunity where you had only seen "crap" before.

After giving crystal healing sessions, two words I hear most in feedback are *clarity* and *healing*. Clients remark how their session has made them see their lives much more clearly. They have allowed the crystals to recalibrate their energies, resulting in a perspective more aligned with their soul's truth, and this causes them to live with more conscientiousness and purpose. Being true to themselves causes them to love themselves more. Without realizing, they begin to interact with others differently, and, in turn, others can't help but treat them differently too. Because a single person changes the central point from which they operate, a cascade of energy occurs that reverberates to everyone they meet.

Crystalline energy is frank and no-nonsense, profound and cathartic, which is why it is so deeply healing. Like the energy of Mother Earth who births them, crystals are full of tough love. But it's a love that cuts to your core in order to help you become the happiest and most fulfilled you can be.

This book will teach you to work with crystalline energy in a conscientious way so that you can use its fierce and powerful energy at a pace and intensity that works best for you. It may not be as dramatic as what you would experience in a guided crystal healing session, but as long as you are willing to work with crystal energies, what you discover can be so powerful that it can profoundly change your life.

La Pietra Paesina (aka Ruin Marble or Florentine Marble)

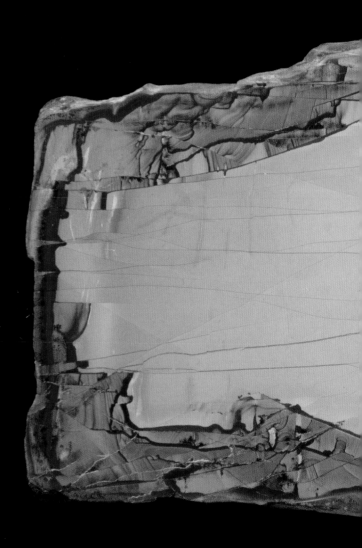

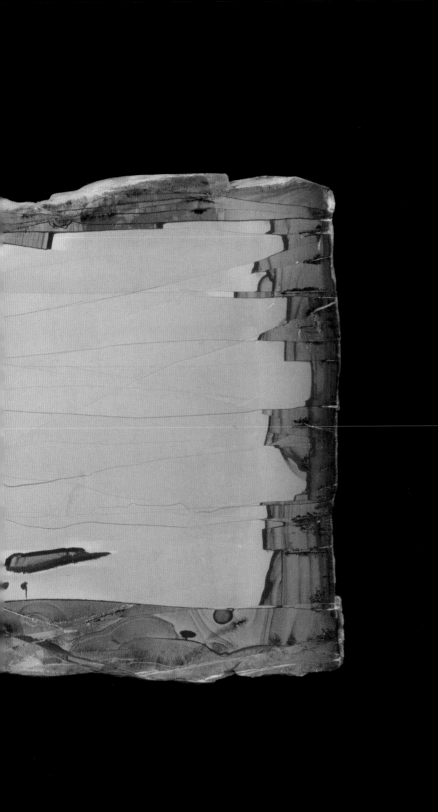

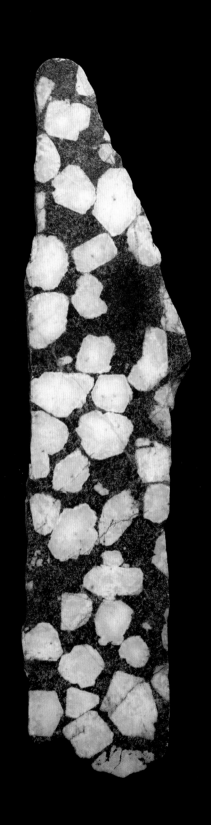

OPPOSITE: Pink Porphyry   ABOVE: Maligano jasper cabochon

CHAPTER 3

THE IMPORTANCE OF THE QUARTZ FAMILY

HAVE YOU EVER looked at a watch and seen the word *quartz* written on its face? You may understand that quartz is a part of the watch, but why is it so important that it gets such high billing, written alongside the watch's brand name?

This is because of the revolutionary way quartz has affected timekeeping.

It used to be that watches were entirely dependent on some mechanical force to keep accurate time. To keep this consistent time, they need something oscillating—something swinging back and forth at a regular speed. For instance, the ticktock of an old grandfather clock is a result of the giant pendulum beneath, swinging rhythmically to and fro, keeping time with its steady oscillations.

One of the miraculous properties of quartz is that it's piezoelectric, meaning that when you apply mechanical stress to it (for example, by squeezing it), it generates an electric charge. This property also works in reverse. If you run an electric current through quartz, the quartz will change shape, as if it's being physically squeezed. Accurately shaping and positioning the quartz, then applying continual electrical energy to it, causes the quartz to oscillate and vibrate in a rhythmic way. And because quartz oscillates with an especially precise and consistent frequency, it is used to keep supremely accurate time in watches.

Although there are other piezoelectric minerals, quartz's abundance and physical stability means that it is the standard timekeeping material around the world. Cell phones, cars, computers, GPS, pressure and temperature sensors, printers, cochlear implants, and heart pacemakers also depend on quartz's precise resonating frequency in order to function. So it is accurate to say that the existence of our modern technological world is based on quartz. But . . .

WHAT EXACTLY *IS* QUARTZ?

When a single silicon atom (Si) bonds with two oxygen atoms (O_2) the result is a molecule called silicon dioxide (SiO_2). The bonding of these three atoms forms a building block that, when stacked and bonded in a coherent and orderly way, creates a crystalline structure known as **quartz**.

Now for a little lesson on silicon and its prevalence on our planet. Also interchangeably called silica, silicon dioxide makes up 15 percent of the Earth's crust. Any mineral that contains any amount of silicon dioxide is called a silicate. The class of silicates includes many different kinds of crystal subclasses including all feldspars, garnets, zircons, rhyolites, flints, tourmalines, zeolites, and more. The next page shows examples of some of these silicates, including chrysocolla [$Cu_2H_2Si_2O5(OH)_4$], andradite garnet [$Ca_3Fe_2Si_3O_{12}$], lepidolite [$K(Li,A_l)_3(Si,A_l)_4O_{10}(F,OH)_2$], phenakite [$Be_2SiO_4$], topaz [$A_{l2}SiO_4(F,OH)_2$], zircon [$ZrSiO_4$], epidote [$\{Ca_2\}\{A_{l2}Fe_3+\}(Si_2O_7)$ $(SiO_4)O(OH)$], sodalite [$Na_8A_{l6}Si_6O_{24}C_{l2}$], and hemimorphite [$Zn_4Si_2O_7(OH)_2$ • H_2O]. Notice how all have some combination of silicon (Si) and oxygen (O). It is the silicate family that makes up over 95 percent of the Earth's crust. This means . . .

We're literally floating on a crystal ball in outer space!

As you now see, much of our planet's crust is derived from some combination of silicon and oxygen, with a significant percentage in the form of quartz.

QUARTZ'S MANY SHAPES AND FORMS

When most people think of quartz, they think of the colorless and translucent variety known as rock crystal. Many people are also familiar with varieties that have quartz in their names, like rose quartz and smoky quartz. But did you know

Examples of silicates, clockwise from
top left: chrysocolla, andradite garnet,
lepidolite, phenakite, topaz, spinel,
epidote, sodalite, hemimorphite

amethyst and citrine are quartzes too? Quartzes like these can become colored when trace minerals are built into their crystal lattice during their growth. Quartz actually comes in hundreds of varieties that differ in color, shape, and size, with new variations discovered every year.

The classic image of quartz is of a colorless, translucent crystal with angular points. When quartz has individual and distinct crystals that can be seen by your naked eye, it fits in a subgroup of quartzes known as macrocrystalline quartz. Examples in this category include clear quartz (aka rock crystal), amethyst, and smoky quartz. But there are also varieties of quartz where the individual crystals are so small they cannot be seen by the naked eye. If you can see the crystals under an optical microscope, then the quartz is considered a microcrystalline quartz. If you need an X-ray or electron microscope to see the individual crystals, it is considered a type of cryptocrystalline quartz.

Here's where the subgroups can get a little confusing (but hang in there with me, because this is helpful background information to know when shopping for crystals): Any rock called an agate, onyx, jasper, aventurine, chert, flint, chrysoprase, or chalcedony is either a micro- or cryptocrystalline quartz. But whether the stone is actually considered micro- or cryptocrystalline depends on if you are using the old or modern classification system. To add even more confusion, people who discover rocks sometimes misidentify them and call a stone, say, a jasper, when in fact it is not. (And these names can stick—as with Dalmatian jasper, which is not truly a jasper because it does not contain any quartz.) However, to simplify this information using the modern classification system, it is precise to call *all* micro- and cryptocrystalline quartzes types of chalcedony.

While macrocrystalline quartzes like amethyst or smoky quartz have a consistent chemical formula throughout the crystal, chalcedonies intermix quartz with other minerals. For example, jaspers are rocks that have fractures and voids filled with other kinds of rocks, while agates have bands of quartz of varying translucency, with layers sometimes picking up color as other minerals become embedded within them. Onyx is really just black-and-white banded agate, though there's been such a long history of using it as a lapidary stone, the name has stuck.

When the same silicon dioxide molecules that make up quartz are not bonded in an orderly structure but are instead connected as a jumble of atoms like Lego blocks randomly attached to one another, they form what is known as an *amorphous solid*. Seventy percent of obsidian, a natural glass created by volcanoes, consists of silicon dioxide in this form. Opal is another form of silicon dioxide in amorphous solid form that is additionally hydrated with water. Because the molecules in opal and obsidian do not have a regularly repeating crystalline structure, they are not considered true minerals but are known as mineraloids.

QUARTZ IN OUR MODERN WORLD

Interestingly, the most common way we encounter amorphous solid silicon dioxide is in manmade products derived from sand. Though sand on tropical beaches is made mostly of ground pieces of coral and shellfish, nontropical sand is made mostly of silicon dioxide (aka silica). Over time, quartz crystals, exposed to weathering, are ground down into small bits of sand, and this silica-rich sand becomes the raw material used to create every manmade glass object you encounter, including glass tumblers, computer and television screens, solar panels, glass-bottled beverages, and every window on every building you see. Glass has special properties that make it uniquely valuable and useful. Not only is glass strong, it can be warped into different shapes while still maintaining the ability to transmit light. It is also nonporous, stable at normal temperatures, and able to resist corrosion, which is why scientific labs use glass in their labware to store hazardous and dangerous materials. Sand also shapes our modern life as a major component of two of the most commonly used construction materials on Earth: concrete and asphalt. Sand, a nonrenewable resource, is in such global demand that it is the second most-used raw material in the world after water, and demand for it continues to rise.

Another huge part of our modern lives is the ubiquitous silicon microchip, a component of virtually every electrical device used by man and on which every computer-related product depends. Silicon too is derived from an ore of, you guessed it—quartz.

Not only do we live on a quartz crystal ball, but it is quartz crystals that make our modern life possible!

QUARTZ IS IMPORTANT

Quartz is extremely common and found on every continent of the world—and that's precisely why it is energetically important. Though quartz is a significant raw material that our modern world depends on, Mother Earth has made quartz widely accessible to us so that we can use it metaphysically. Despite all the hype that can surround rarer and harder-to-find crystals, they are not the crystals metaphysically needed the most. Mother Earth has purposefully set things up so the crystals most helpful to you are the same crystals that are easiest to access. Thus, the globally available quartz and quartz-based crystals are the core of your personal crystal healing tool kit.

QUARTZ: THE PREMIER PROGRAMMING CRYSTAL

In 2016, researchers at the University of Southampton developed a form of digital data storage that laser-inscribed information onto quartz glass. Each one-inch disk holds the equivalent of 360 terabytes of information, which would amount to over 121 million copies of *War and Peace* or over seventy-six thousand DVDs! Not only does the quartz glass hold incredible amounts of information, each disk has an estimated life span of 13.8 billion years—which is over three times the current age of the Earth, and almost the entire age of the physical universe itself!

Modern science is continuing to discover more about the amazing physical properties of quartz, but the incredible power of this crystal was something the ancients already knew. From the sacred jewelry of the Egyptians to crystal divination practiced by the Greeks and Romans to the quartz artifacts buried all over the world, quartz has long been used in mystic ceremonies all around the planet.

One of the more captivating uses of quartz in the ancient world was with crystal skulls. Most closely associated with Mesoamerican tribes, crystal skulls are also known to be used by Tibetan Buddhist monks. Though the two cultural groups come from opposite sides of the world, spiritual leaders from both say these skulls are ancient and sacred repositories of cosmic information and that they act as record-keepers, observing the world and recording the history of humanity as the eons pass. Current descendants of the ancient Maya see quartz as a kind of supernatural device, similar to that of an ancient radio, television, or computer, in that it acts as a mechanism to facilitate communication between this world and the world of the spirits and ancestors. Modern practitioners who work with crystal skulls explain that the geometry of the human skull holds unique cosmic properties that become enhanced when this geometry is replicated in quartz. They report that the crystal skulls amplify quartz's ability to work as a recording device, which supports the statements made by Mesoamericans and Tibetans. In addition to their ability to record and communicate, crystal skulls are said to possess healing ability.

Though crystal skulls are powerful, quartz does not need to be in the shape of a skull in order for you to access its incredible properties, for even quartz in its original state is still the premier programming crystal.

MARCEL VOGEL

Marcel Joseph Vogel (1917–91) was a brilliant scientist whose discoveries helped propel modern technology as we now know it. His lifelong research into phosphorescence influenced popular culture through his development of the fluorescent paints that defined the look of the '60s. He was also responsible for creating black-light technology and discovering applications for it including cancer detection. Later in his career he spent twenty-seven years working at IBM as a research scientist in their prestigious Advanced Systems Development lab, where he pioneered the understanding of liquid crystal displays (used in everything from calculators to televisions) as well as the creation of the revolutionary magnetic coating that is still used on hard drives today. By the end of his tenure at IBM, Vogel's accomplishments also included thirty-two patents filed in the fields of luminescence, phosphor technology, magnetics, and liquid crystal systems. After retiring from IBM, and still insatiably curious, he opened his own laboratory. There, he would go on to research bioenergetic fields and energetically structured water.

During this time Vogel also stumbled upon a discovery that would captivate him for the rest of his life. While conducting experiments intended to study communication between humans and plants, he accidentally discovered that the quartz in his lab was reacting to the same experiments and was responding to the humans' bioenergetic fields as well. This led him to dedicate much of his research to quartz, for in it he found a structurally perfect material that could be directly programmed to hold vibrations of thought and intent that could be used for healing. Vogel would go on to declare the quartz crystal to be "a neutral object whose inner structure exhibits a state of perfection and balance" and that "when the human mind enters into relationship with its structural perfection, the crystal emits a vibration which extends and amplifies the power of the user's mind."

This is why quartz is such a powerful stone, for it is an **amplifier of vibration**. Though Vogel's research on quartz specifically focused on amplifying the power of the mind, quartz's inherent neutrality and ability to "turbo-boost" vibrations means that it will amplify any vibration put into it.

TURBO-BOOSTING WITH QUARTZ

On an atomic level, quartz is made up of pyramid-shaped building blocks consisting of silicon and oxygen. These atomic pyramids (technically called tetrahedrons) stack on top of each other in rows of spirals that converge to a point at the tip of a crystal (see next page). As energy moves through the crystal, it follows this helix pattern in the quartz crystalline lattice. And just like a roller coaster gaining momentum on a spiraling track, the energy moving through the quartz gains velocity as it moves through the spirals.

Think of the spirals found in nature: Hurricanes and tornadoes increasing in intensity as their giant spirals whirl across the Earth, black holes with vortexes so powerful they distort both gravity and time. There is even a spiral of water that helps you flush your toilet! The energy in a spiral is powerful because it leads and concentrates energy to a specific point, which creates the "turbo-boosting" of energies. And it is this property within quartz that makes it a very powerful stone.

An idealized version of a left-handed quartz with a counterclockwise spiral of molecules. (Quartz can also be right-handed, with a clockwise-turning spiral of molecules.) For visual clarity this illustration shows just one spiral, but in actuality each column has two spirals wrapping around each other, creating a double helix—just like our DNA.

This is why you must be careful about where quartz is placed.

Because quartz is energetically neutral, it amplifies any vibration around it, including negative electromagnetic frequencies (EMFs) coming from your electronics on a subtle level.

Have you had the experience of standing close to a power line or electric transformer, hearing and feeling its weird buzz vibrating though you? It's not a pleasant experience. EMFs from electronics also create the same kind of buzzing on a metaphysically energetic level, but because most electronics are much smaller, they vibrate on a much lower "volume." But if you place quartz next to your electronics, you amplify their EMF energies and "turn up" this volume energetically. You may not notice the effects on a physical level, but your energetic bodies can be affected by them in ways that can cascade into your physical experience. As cool as a quartz crystal looks on your desk, if placed close to your computer it will magnify the negative EMFs coming off it. And since your computer can be a place where you feel stressed, the quartz will also amplify your stress and any other negative feelings you may be experiencing near it. This same advice applies to cell phones. If you keep your phone by your bed next to a quartz crystal, the interaction of the cell phone EMFs amplified by the quartz crystal will create energies that are disruptive to your sleep.

Solution: Move the quartz away from electronics.

Try this out: If you're keeping your quartz by your computer, move the quartz across the room and away from any electronics. Then go back to your computer, reimmerse yourself in your work, and forget that you've moved the crystal. When you take a break and finally remember that your crystal is no longer at your desk, notice how you feel. Do you feel different than you did before you moved it? Has your work been going more smoothly? The results can be quite surprising. I have had many people try this experiment and report significant drops in stress levels, an increase in productivity, and the experience of difficult projects suddenly coming together, just because they moved their quartz crystal away from the electronics on their desks.

You can try this experiment the other way around too: Place a quartz crystal next to your computer for a few days and see how you end up feeling. You may not notice anything at first because you will quickly acclimate to the quartz's energy. But after a few days, put the quartz away, and see if you feel any different once it's no longer sitting at your desk. The instantaneous drop in stress levels is always nice.

You can do a similar experiment if you have been sleeping next to both a quartz crystal and your phone. Move the phone out of the room, or at least to the part of your room farthest away from your bed. Take notice of any improvement in your sleep. You will likely find that you are sleeping better than you were before.

I will talk more about programming your quartz crystals to help direct their energy in a particular, chosen direction in chapter 12. But even if your crystal is programmed, know that I would still avoid keeping quartz crystals next to electronics. There are other crystals better suited as desk or bed crystals, including ones that will be explained in the next chapter.

Because quartz is indiscriminate about what it amplifies, you also need to be cautious about wearing it in jewelry. Now that crystals have become so popular, I often see people wearing quartz jewelry. But not only will the quartz amplify any EMF energies coming out of a cell phone kept in your pocket or held in your hand, it will also amplify any negative feelings or thoughts you may have. So even if you are feeling confident on the outside, if you have any hidden or subconscious thoughts bouncing inside your head criticizing you or telling you you're not good enough, the energy of those thoughts will become magnified by the quartz. Even worse, if you are suppressing or trying to ignore this kind of thought energy, it will prevent the energy from releasing and resolving and instead make it grow larger. Energetically, denial is like trying to pack a large amount of clothes into a very small suitcase. The energy can never be completely locked up, for it will always spill at the seams. And if the suitcase gets any sliver of an opening (especially when it's opened up a crack so more denial can be added into it), it will burst. Add some unprogrammed quartz, and it's like adding some explosives to the suitcase too!

Even more concerning is when people wear quartz point pendants with the point facing down toward their feet. This means they are sending accelerated energy from out-of-alignment thoughts down from their mind toward their lower chakras. Then, the solar plexus, which governs emotion, may translate this energy as negative feelings, while the root chakra may pick up the energy and perceive it as a lack of physical security. Then, in a bad feedback loop, the mind responds to the experiences of the lower chakras with more anxiety, sending the person further on a downward spiral of energy. Unbeknownst to the wearer, the crystal point around their neck has been intensifying their insecurities this whole time.

Because quartz energy has so much power, you don't want to work with it in an unconscious way. You want to work with crystals to support your highest energies of love, fulfillment, and happiness. But that's why you're reading this book, right?

MAIN KINDS OF QUARTZ

While all quartzes have turbo-boosting spirals within their crystal lattice, different varieties will cause the amplifying energies to be projected in a particular direction. The following are the most common quartz varieties used in crystal healing, each with its own "flavor" for what it is energetically inclined to do.

Clear Quartz

Also known as rock crystal, this type of quartz is translucent and colorless and most often found as a crystal point or cluster of crystal points. Because it does not contain any other chemical elements or minerals that shift its color, it is the most energetically neutral quartz to work with.

While colored crystals have a specific focus for their energies, clear quartz is like a blank sheet of white paper and thus has an unlimited range of what can be programmed into it. This makes clear quartz the ultimate programming stone as well as the ideal stone to use for turbo-boosting the energies of other stones.

Amethyst

You know when you walk into a spa and notice that the air smells different? Minute particles of essential oils and moisture escape the treatment rooms, ever so faintly scenting the air with their calming aroma. Even if you focused only on this one subtle detail, you would still be able to recognize how the smell demarcates the space of the spa from the world outside. This is the energy of amethyst. It is energy that is subtle and very quiet, and like the faint smell that lets you know you are in a different place, the energy of amethyst subtly shifts the energetic space around you and gently eases you into the spiritual worlds.

Amethyst is a gateway stone. When people begin their journey connecting with the crystals, amethyst is often the first stone they find themselves especially attracted to. And it makes sense, since amethyst is a stone that helps you become more aware of the spiritual worlds.

Working with amethyst is similar to turning on the radio and discovering a station you didn't realize was even available. As you tune in to its frequency, you are able to connect to a tone of energy that you had not known was there before, which is the higher, more subtle frequency of the spiritual worlds.

Instead of other crystals that can forcefully fling you into intense third-eye journeys, amethyst creates a soft and gentle space for you to experience spirituality. So if you are interested in delving deeper into the spiritual dimensions and do not have the assistance of an experienced healer, or do not yet possess the metaphysical skills to navigate these dimensions' more potent aspects, it's best to begin your journey into the spiritual worlds in a gentle way, for this will minimize any trauma you would experience by going too deep and fast before you were prepared to do so.

If you are already familiar with traveling the spiritual worlds, amethyst is a perfect stone to use for a relatively more gentle and leisurely jaunt into the spiritual dimensions than what you might experience with other stones or modalities.

Rose Quartz

In the next chapter I'll go into more depth about the significance of rose quartz, but for the time being know that rose quartz is the stone that most closely resonates with the vibration of pure love.

Rose quartz is most commonly found as simple and humble semiopaque chunks of rough pink rock. Often mistaken as a stone of romance, the healing energy of rose quartz does not specifically apply to any particular kind of relationship. Instead, rose quartz represents love in its most basic and essential form. It's the energy of love when it's undramatic, constant, and secure. It is a love for all relationships, including love of self.

Because there is no situation that could not use more love, rose quartz is an infinitely useful stone.

Citrine

Real citrine is most often a softly tinted yellow or greenish yellow stone with brown undertones, frequently imbued with smoky gray hues. Though it is most popularly known as a manifestation stone especially as it relates to money, this is only a cursory understanding of citrine's metaphysical properties. While citrine does resonate with manifestation and can help with manifesting more money, money problems themselves are more than likely related to the root chakra (which I will explain in the next chapter). But because citrine is so popularly associated with money manifestation, it stays in high demand.

However, true citrine is actually quite rare and not easy to come by. To meet demand, citrine is often artificially manufactured by heat-treating amethyst, which results in a "citrine" with a dark orangey-yellow hue. I'll go more into depth about artificial citrine in chapter 6, but in the meantime I suggest avoiding using citrine that has this hypersaturated hue.

If, however, you are able to get the real citrine, it is a wonderful stone to help facilitate manifestation by giving a turbo-boost both to your willpower and to the energy around whatever idea you want to manifest.

Smoky Quartz

When clear quartz is buried in the ground, it can receive natural radiation from Mother Earth. This radiation changes the color of the quartz from clear to a black-hued form of varying opacities known as smoky quartz. Smoky quartz can also be found in combination with other types of quartz where it can create faint wisps of smokiness within amethyst or citrine crystals.

Further explanation of the root chakra will appear in the next chapter, but in the meantime know that smoky quartz increases the capacity for spiritual light to enter the root chakra, which is especially useful for those who have root chakras that have become energetically dense. This heaviness of the root chakra can be a result of feeling mired by physical life—for instance, when one feels as if one is continually slogging through one's day-to-day existence—or experiencing life-threatening health issues that drain one's physical strength. Smoky quartz will strengthen the root chakra on a grass-roots level by giving an energetic boost to a person's life force. And, because of its natural exposure to radiation, smoky quartz is excellent for helping people get energetically acclimated to any radiative treatment, including chemotherapy.

But as with citrine, be aware that artificially created smoky quartz is prevalent. Unlike real smoky quartz, the color of artificially treated smoky quartz is a sharp and shiny black, especially toward the crystal's tips. I'll go into more information about artificially treated crystals in chapter 6, but in the meantime avoid this type of smoky quartz, as it does more energetic harm than good.

Quartz

OPPOSITE: Quartz with specular hematite   ABOVE: Quartz with hematite

Agate slice

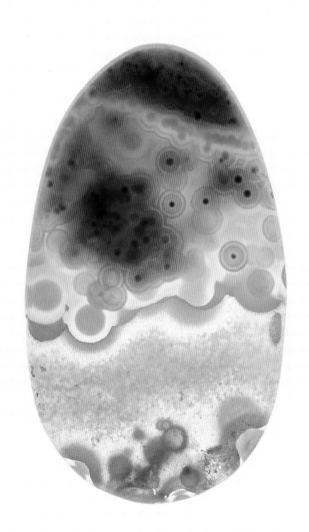

Ocean Jasper

"In a crystal we have the clear evidence
of the existence of a formative life-
principle, and though we cannot
understand the life of a crystal—it is
nonetheless still a living being."
—Nikola Tesla

OPPOSITE: Quartz Chalcedony

ABOVE: Gold Sheen Obsidian
(aka Mahogany Obsidian)

CHAPTER 4

THE ESSENTIAL
THREE

WHILE THE IMMENSE DIVERSITY and wide availability of the quartz family make it an exceedingly resourceful group of stones to use for crystal healing, it is but one species in the mineral kingdom. There are thousands of minerals, each one containing varieties and subvarieties too. Out of this great breadth of mineral diversity, three stones stand out for their all-around metaphysical usefulness and versatility.

Much as salt, pepper, and cooking oil are staples in your kitchen, I recommend the stones I describe in this chapter as the staples of your crystal kit because of their ability to assist you with a wide variety of energetic needs. These stones are so useful that if you purchase only three stones, these would be the ones I recommend. So if you're just beginning to work with crystals, I suggest that you acquire these first. And if you already have a collection of crystals, these are stones you want to make sure are in your crystal kit. As you read on, you'll understand why.

BLACK TOURMALINE

In mineral circles, tourmaline is jokingly called the "mineral garbage can" because it so willingly accepts such a wide variety of other elements into its crystal lattice. This makes tourmaline one of the most chemically complicated groups in the silicate family and accounts for the dramatic range of colors it comes in.

Specifically, black tourmaline (also called schorl) is tourmaline with iron in its lattice (take note: iron is going to make a significant appearance again) and is the

Black Tourmaline

most common variety of tourmaline found on Earth. Black tourmaline is also what I like to call the energetic "first line of defense" because of how exceptional it is for dealing with the negativity found in ordinary everyday life.

Having a bad day?	*Black tourmaline.*
Someone cut you off and gave you the finger?	*Black tourmaline.*
Heard some upsetting news?	*Black tourmaline.*
Planning to have a possibly complicated conversation with someone?	*Black tourmaline.*
Work hectic and stressful?	*Black tourmaline.*
Got weird energies floating around the room? Like the energetic remnants of some big fight or a creepy ghost-like vibe that gives you the chills?	*Black tourmaline.*
Giving yourself a stream of negative self-talk?	*Black tourmaline.*
Broke your toe?	*Black tourmaline.*
Mercury in retrograde?	*Black tourmaline.*

Black tourmaline. Black tourmaline. Black tourmaline.

Though you can find many descriptions of black tourmaline calling it a "shield for negativity," I find this wording a bland and slightly inaccurate way to describe the properties of this very valuable stone. This is because the magic of black tourmaline is not about "defending" you, but rather its amazing ability to recycle negative energy into positive energy!

Like quartz, tourmaline is piezoelectric so, when squeezed, it develops an electrical charge. But unlike quartz, tourmaline develops its electric charge along its length. One end of the stone will have a positive charge while the other end has a negative one, like the ends of a battery. This inclination to create polarity on a physical level is also reflected on a subtle level, allowing a tourmaline to take in negative energy on one end and then transform it into positive energy on the other! This means **any** energetic crap in your life can be turned into nourishing, healing compost! And because black tourmaline is particularly associated with life in the physical dimension, it is the ideal tourmaline to help you take what's energetically terrible in your life and flip it into something useful for you.

Understanding this one attribute helps you to perceive the opportunities and benefits in even the worst of situations while working with this stone. Black tourmaline teaches you to see pathways that can allow you to move toward a happier and more empowered space, rather than getting stuck in negativity. So instead of worrying about negative energy being hurled at you, bonking you on the head, and leaving you with some nasty energetic bump, with black tourmaline you are able to catch negativity like a ball and transform it into energy you can use beneficially. With this information, you are empowered with the knowledge that you have the ability to shift any energy that comes toward you rather than resign yourself to be a victim of circumstance. This is why I call black tourmaline the "first line of defense."

However, there is an even deeper level to understand about the transformation of negative energy into positive energy. While it's true that black tourmaline shifts negative energy into positive energy, what it is actually doing is bringing unbalanced energy into an equalized state. In algebra, if you add a positive 1 to a negative 1, the result equals zero ($+1 + -1 = 0$). In the same way, the addition of an equal amount of positive energy to negative energy ultimately brings the energy into a state of balance where it is neither pushing into positivity nor pulling into negativity. This same principle happens with the energy that is around you when you work with black tourmaline. If you are dealing with negative energy, you will need positive energy to bring the situation into a balanced state.

This also means that if you have an excess of positive energy around you, you will need negative energy to balance it out. While it is a common belief that "positive" energy means "good" energy, and "negative" energy means "bad" energy, this is not necessarily true. From a higher, spiritual point of view, energy is not divided into two separate categories; for all energy is part of the Universe, and everything in the Universe serves a purpose impelling you toward greater spiritual evolvement. Thus, from this nondualistic standpoint, there is no "bad" energy—just energy that is out of balance. But humans have an inclination to organize things into categories because this creates a sense of order and predictability. So humans will organize energy as being "good" or "bad," when in each case the designation is a personal call

Black tourmaline in quartz cabochon

of judgment. Either way, the reason the energy can be labeled as "good" or "bad" is that it sticks out in some way. This indicates that the energy is skewed toward one pole and is flowing in an imbalanced way.

For energy to flow at its best, it needs to be in a balanced state, and because the majority of life's situations are skewed toward negativity, it is positive energy that is most often needed to bring balance to a situation. So while it's true that black tourmaline recycles negative energy into positive energy, it does not do so exclusively. Black tourmaline will transform any energy that needs to come into balance, no matter how it's labeled, in order to create an optimal energetic flow.

How Black Tourmaline Can Help

The following are specific situations where black tourmaline can be powerfully used to assist you in balancing polarities.

ON YOUR DESK, NEXT TO YOUR COMPUTER

Nowadays, computers are ubiquitous and requisite tools for life. Since they are the main tools of modern communication and productivity, the experience of being on a computer can contain some degree of stress—and sometimes quite a lot of it, especially when it comes to work. Because most people work on a computer at some sort of desk, this becomes an ideal place to interact closely with a stone that has a profound ability to shift stress and negative energies into positive ones, which will make your work life more productive.

Remember in the previous chapter when I said not to keep quartz next to your computer because of the way it magnifies all energies, including bad moods and EMFs (see page 75)? Well, unlike quartz and most other minerals, black tourmaline is one of the few crystals I can recommend keeping at your desk. Its ability to change polarities makes this stone your most useful ally in the workplace.

Keep your black tourmaline somewhere on your desk where you can easily see it. That way every time you glance at it you can be reminded of its ability to recycle energies, while remembering to stay open and accepting of its support. If you feel you are in need of extra support, you can also physically hold the stone, for instance when you're on a tough phone call, in a challenging meeting, or working on a diffi-cult project. Take whatever negative energies you are feeling and channel them into the stone in your hand. This allows you to communicate and energetically transfer to the stone what exact energies or situations you would like support transforming. Then feel yourself absorbing the balanced energy now being produced by the stone, and observe how this shift in energy affects you personally. At first, the shift may seem very subtle, perhaps just the slightest change in your demeanor or attitude, but once you recognize the movement happening, quietly observe how the situation changes. You will be surprised by how a tiny shift can make such a noticeable change for the better in your environment.

FOR NIGHTMARES AND RESTLESS SLEEP

The combination of black tourmaline's grounding energies and its ability to help recycle negative situations into positive ones makes it an excellent stone for those having trouble sleeping because of restless thoughts or nightmares.

Smaller pieces of black tourmaline, like pocket, tumbled-size pieces, can be placed in your pillowcase. Larger, more substantial pieces can be placed in bed and slept with, allowing the black tourmaline to act as your personal cuddly teddy bear/ energetic defensive linebacker. If the kind of black tourmaline you have is prone to flaking, instead of sleeping with it and having it shed splintered pieces all over your bed, just place it somewhere near you, like your bed stand, while you sleep. As long as it's close to your body, it will be within your aura where its energies can support you.

While black tourmaline can help mitigate negative EMFs from electronics, it's still best to keep electronics away from you while you're sleeping. Otherwise, your black tourmaline will have to split its energy over multiple tasks rather than focusing all its energy on caring for you. While I strongly recommend keeping your phone and other electronics outside your bedroom, if that is not possible then keep them across the room, as far from your bed and stone as you can.

If you're concerned about negative energies coming into your house, place black tourmaline at the entryways. Then set an intention for the stones to keep out anyone with negative aims from coming into your home. You can also use black tourmaline to help keep your home as your sanctuary by setting an intention for the negativity of the world to stay outside and not come through your doors. Though the black tourmaline will not keep all negativity from coming in (because negativity can still be self-generated after crossing the threshold of your doors), it can help you be more aware of negativity so you can be more proactive in keeping it out.

Other Notes on Black Tourmaline

If someone were to ask me what crystal I use most in terms of quantity, I would answer, "Black tourmaline." I have it on my desk at home, on my desk at work, by my bed, guarding my house, and in my car, and it is one of the stones I most consistently wear. I even have a travel kit of black tourmalines I take on trips with me to help recycle the energy of spaces I stay in, as well as guard against any negative energies bothering me (including any lost spirits that may be in the building where I am staying). It's a stone so useful I have it peppered everywhere.

It's best to have different black tourmalines for different jobs. If you have a black tourmaline at your desk, designate it as your desk tourmaline and keep it there. If you have a black tourmaline to help with your sleeping, designate that specific one as your sleeping tourmaline. Having multiple black tourmalines ensures you will have them where you need them, when you need them, at all times. Having multiple black tourmalines helps them from overloading because of all crystals, black tourmaline is most famous for sacrificing itself for the people it cares for.

One of my favorite stories about this comes from a friend and colleague of mine. Black tourmaline is *her* stone, meaning that of all minerals it's the one that resonates most deeply with her on a constitutional level. She was once in the middle of a very intense conversation with her partner when she suddenly heard and felt a pop on her chest. Immediately knowing that it was her beloved black tourmaline she wore around her neck, she caught it in her hand as it exploded into pieces. Like an overloaded fuse, her black tourmaline took the brunt of negative energy being released as deep wounds became surfaced during her conversation, and it sacrificed itself in order to protect her.

Many others have told me similar stories of their perfectly intact black tourmalines suddenly crumbling on them. I even had one client who was sitting on her bed when from the corner of her eye she saw her black tourmaline spontaneously shatter on her bed stand. Because so much negativity can surround daily life and because it quietly handles so much volume, black tourmaline tends to get overworked. When it does, it can break into pieces or just stop working.

While this doesn't apply to all stones, bigger is better when it comes to black tourmaline. A larger stone will have a greater recycling capacity and ability to handle larger amounts of energy. But more important than having a larger specimen is regularly cleansing it, for this is what allows it to work optimally (cleansing will be explained in chapter 10). While for energetic capacity and portability I most often recommend a size that can fit substantially in your hand, if you don't have a larger tourmaline yet, it is fine to work with multiple smaller ones, as long as you're cleansing them often.

For general help with processing negativity, you can simply carry black tourmaline. The closer to you it is, the better its energy can interact with yours, so one good place to put it is in your pocket. That way it can support you as you encounter negative energies when going about your daily life. Or imagine any place or situation where you deal with a lot of negativity and place a black tourmaline at that location to help you.

As you continue working with black tourmaline's energy, you will see all the different ways it can help you, and this will encourage you to figure out new ways to apply its helpful energies. Just remember that black tourmaline is here to teach you that shifting the polarity of energy to your benefit is *always* possible.

Black Tourmalines

Hematite pseudomorph after magnetite,
above a streak of ocher

HEMATITE

Hematite has always been important to humanity.

Even though our Stone Age ancestors had charcoal left over from their fires to draw with, they traveled long distances to collect hematite. They then took great effort to process it into the pigment known as ocher. In addition to painting scenes of their ancient lives on cave walls all over the world, our ancient ancestors used this pigment to decorate jewelry made of bones and teeth, as well as to decorate funerary material in burials. And now, even after hundreds of thousands of years, it is still being used in indigenous rituals to symbolize blood, the principle of life.

When hematite is scraped, it produces a rusty red powder, which, when mixed with a bit of water, looks like blood. This is why the ancient Greeks named the stone *hematite,* literally translated as "blood stone." When the iron in hematite combines with the oxygen in the air it produces the red color we see. In fact, this same synergy of iron and oxygen occurs within ourselves as well. Our bodies produce an iron-containing protein, hemoglobin, which carries the oxygen we breathe and transports it through our bloodstream to oxygenate the rest of our body. Hemoglobin is what makes the color of our blood red and is what allows our body to breathe and live. The iron within our blood is thus essential to our physical survival.

Both literally and figuratively, blood represents what keeps our bodies alive. And conversely, its absence in our body represents death. This relationship between blood and life is what our ancient ancestors saw all around them. They knew that hunting an animal and eating its bloody flesh allowed the one who caught it to live. While the female sex had the magic to create completely new life from within her body, from this same place she was also endowed with the mystic ability to regularly bleed and shed her life essence without dying. In these very significant ways, our ancestors experienced how blood was the medium of life and death.

The Root Chakra

This focus on life and death is precisely the realm of the root chakra. The Sanskrit word for root chakra is *muladhara*, a combination of *mula*, "root," and *adhara*, "support" or "base." Located at the base (or "root") of your spine, this chakra governs life's first needs of physical survival.

When a baby is born, the very first things it requires to live are food, shelter, and warmth. And if these primal requirements are not met, the baby will die—the experiences of emotion, of love, and of intellect will have no foundation on which to exist. Human connection becomes irrelevant.

Physical survival then means that the most essential requirements to live are met. It means depending on the surrounding environment to provide you with all the materials needed to live, as well as the ability to take action with them to further create scenarios that support your ability to survive. Since Mother Earth provides food, shelter, and warmth for all her creatures, survival means depending on her and working with her so that you may live.

Any healthy ecosystem in nature demonstrates this. Though there exists a constant dynamic between life and death, the ecosystem still teems with the vibrancy of life. All its beings live in synergy, using only the raw materials provided by Mother Earth. These healthy ecosystems, with their lush expression of life, project resiliency and, inherent in this, the sense that Mother Earth provides everything that is needed to survive, even for the smallest of her creatures.

Likewise, when humans have a healthy relationship with their root chakra, they feel confident and safe about their physical lives. They do not worry about their most basic needs of living, for they know that everything they need to survive can be found on Mother Earth. This expectation that Mother Earth already has the resources all beings require to live is why animals are the greatest teachers of the lessons of the root chakra. They live their life in the moment dealing with their primal needs as necessary. They catch food to eat when they are hungry, sun themselves when they want to warm up, and dig holes and make burrows when they desire shelter. They don't worry about time but are present with their needs in the moment, for their internal rhythms are harmonized with the energetic patterns of Mother Earth's

Hematite

cycles so they always know when it's the right time to take another action. And because animals implicitly know there are always ways to survive, it never occurs to them to give up and quit. Despite any odds against them, they will do whatever they can to keep going, surviving, creating new generations of life, for they live with the expectation that there is always some way to stay alive.

This is the essence of *grounding*. To be grounded you must be aware of your primal physical self, your relationship to physical nourishment and all things representing shelter and warmth. To be grounded means being connected to Mother Earth, working with her, and knowing that she has everything you need to survive. To be grounded means to be connected and balanced with these energies in your root chakra.

Mother Earth's Root Chakra

While hematite has always been known as a grounding stone, modern technology reaffirms just how significant our relationship to the grounding energy of iron is.

Scientists have discovered that the center of the Earth is a solid iron ball. This means *Mother Earth's root chakra is literally made of iron*! Our most valuable and useful root chakra stone is what actually constitutes her root chakra!

There is a dynamic in Mother Earth's root chakra that is of great significance as well: Surrounding her solid core of iron is a layer of liquid iron. As the liquid iron churns around her solid iron center, it creates our planet's magnetic field, and this field is what keeps our planet intact. It surrounds the entire Earth, acting as a protective shield, deflecting charged particles that flow from the sun on solar winds. Without it, our atmosphere, along with all our oceans and all our air, would be stripped away into outer space.

So can you see why hematite's energy makes it one of the most essential stones for your crystal kit?

The Importance of Grounding

The way modern life is structured disconnects us from nature. We use clocks to schedule our day. We ride in vehicles to get to work. We box ourselves inside climate-controlled environments. We make our dinners from containers and packages we buy at the supermarket. We do so many little things out of convenience and habit, but over time they separate us from our connection to Mother Earth.

While plants and animals stay in tune with the rhythms and cycles of Mother Earth in order to survive and thrive, we depend on modern systems to take care of our physical needs, and this dependency has caused us to fall out of touch with the planet we live upon. The more we rely on technology, the less compelled we are to pay attention to the environment around us. This causes us to lose sensitivity to the information Mother Earth communicates to us through her body. Though she constantly sends us messages and signals, we have no idea that she's even reaching out to us. So while animals will run for higher ground because they have heard her saying that a tsunami is about to hit, we remain clueless that anything is about to happen even though our bodies are also made to hear her.

We forget that we learn a lot about the world around us through touch. Information about an object can be gained simply by touching it with our fingers, for they are so sensitive they can distinguish a pattern within a smooth surface only thirteen nanometers deep, while also differentiating textures, materials, temperatures, and vibrations. We also communicate through touch, and the palms of our hands are among our most powerful tools for giving and receiving information. Whether by a gentle hand on your shoulder, or by someone rubbing your back, cupping your face, or holding your hand, the feelings of care, support, and love can be communicated through touch. Through touch, volumes of information can be given and received. So imagine what your life would be like if you constantly wore gloves. Though you would be touching things, the feeling of them would be muddled and the information you picked up about them would be imprecise. Your sense would not be accurate.

But this is what we do with our feet. In the same way that we use the palms of our hands to communicate and understand the world around us, we use the soles of our feet to communicate and understand the ground beneath us. The soles of our feet have the same sensitivity as the palms of our hands, but because we insulate our feet in shoes we lose touch with information that could be transmitted through them. We lose our ability to communicate with Mother Earth.

Imagine what would happen if a child was never able to feel the touch of a strong and safe maternal body. The world would feel horrid, cold, and unsafe, and on many levels the child would suffer from the lack of touch. Yet this is what we do by wearing shoes. We are the ones who have inadvertently rejected our mother, and we are the ones who suffer without her touch. In the seemingly mundane action of wearing shoes, we have disrupted a vital connection between ourselves and our planet. For it is through bare feet that we are able to connect skin to skin with Mother Earth. And through this contact, we are able to receive the information and energy she always provides for us.

Another way we become disconnected from Mother Earth and ungrounded is with our minds. The *mind* is like a software program in your mental body. Its original purpose is to help you survive by perceiving and evaluating situations in an accurate way to support your soul for its highest good. But while you were in the womb, before you were even born, the mind decided that it wanted to be in control and took over. It decided that "it" was your entire being. To protect itself, it always made itself "right," and to do this it separated you from your direct experience by having you lose touch with your body and emotions.

The mind's belief that it is always "right" is reinforced by a cultural obsession with the cerebral. The modern world has become convinced that the brain is the superior organ and values intellect, logic, reason—all forms of thinking—as the best way to evaluate the world. However, this belief only encourages us to be carried away by our thoughts. We are already unbalanced from our physical disconnection from Mother Earth, but we make things worse by directing too much energy into our minds.

When we believe that we need to give the mind all the control, it sets up a scenario for excess energy to remain around the head. The mind then hoards the energy and keeps it from moving freely into the other chakras where the energy can be better processed. This is a problem because the chakra best positioned to counterbalance the mind's surplus of energy is the chakra farthest from the head—the root chakra.

How an excess of mind energy will appear to clairvoyants differs, but for me the overabundance causes a person's head to look like an overinflated balloon. If they are particularly ungrounded, their balloon head will look as if it is attached to a flimsy, anemic string of a body. Because their other chakras have no "weight" to counteract what's going on in the head, any thought that begins to run around in the mind will cause the person to become unanchored. And just like an untethered balloon, they will be carried away by their thoughts, continually splitting hairs and worrying about outcomes that bear no relationship with reality. For when a mind is in conflict with the root chakra it will think it is doing what is best for your survival, but it's not connected to reality.

But connecting to the root chakra allows energy to be released from the mind. Because the root chakra is located farthest from the mind, connecting to it means that energy must pass through all the other chakras to get to it. As this energy moves downward, the flow of energy causes the chakras to become activated, creating a pathway that relinks all the chakras. So as your energy becomes more evenly balanced across them, you no longer look like an oversize balloon on a string.

The concept of "work" also has a significant effect on the root chakra. This is because "work" is how we get money, and money is what we use in the modern world to survive. Though we use money to pay our bills, buy food, and keep a roof over our heads, we forget that "money" is a symbol, abstracted into colored pieces of paper. We also attempt to translate our feelings about a product or service, along with the effort that was put into it, into a numerical value. But because "effort" and "feelings" are immaterial, they intrinsically have no physical worth. However, we still ascribe numbers to objects because in our modern world this makes it easier to trade goods.

We forget that Mother Earth has always provided for all her creatures. So when our minds forget that we always have her to depend on for our most basic needs, and instead believe that money is the only way to survive, the result is that the mind hoards an excess of mental energy, the root chakra becomes neglected and unbalanced, and we develop a skewed relationship with money.

Though other chakras influence money issues, understanding the root chakra is crucial in understanding them. So while there is a widespread belief that manifestation (an expression of the navel chakra) is all that is needed to make and have money in one's life, this is a fallacy. While the navel chakra does influence the generation of

Hematite geode

money, challenges generating it are not why people have money problems. For even if you were able to manifest lots of money, you could still be dealing with profound fears for your own survival.

For example, if someone blatantly shows off their money, they are attempting to subconsciously convey their ability to survive better than someone else. But they have this desire to overtly demonstrate their worth because they are overcompensating for their own profound internal feelings of lack. This is why an exceedingly wealthy person can still be manically compelled to make far more money than they could ever spend. If you look deep down, their drive stems from insecurities about survival, for they believe the more money they have, the more they will be insulated from any primal experiences of want (not realizing that their obsessive concern actually puts them in a constant state of primal desperation).

Root chakra issues can also affect one's relationship with money through poverty consciousness. If you believe money is "bad," then its existence can only cause harm. Thus you will conclude that any kind of financial success can only be achieved by hurting someone else. This can lead you to deny opportunities for your upliftment because you believe that you must hurt someone else to make your life better. Also, you may believe that success is limited and comes from a finite pool of energy. You will resent those who have money because you will assume that it was stripped from someone else in order for them to have it. Poverty consciousness can also result from feelings of unworthiness. On the surface you may not be aware of it, but you can have subconscious beliefs that you are not deserving of abundance. Deep inside, you may think you are not special enough in God's eyes to be allotted the resources to survive. So, to confirm this belief, you create a self-fulfilling prophecy of lack. You can also experience poverty consciousness as a way to make yourself feel alive, for the struggle to live can stimulate the root chakra out of stagnation, though in a potentially imbalanced and detrimental way.

As nature shows us in healthy ecosystems, there is nothing wrong or bad about surviving well and with abundance on Mother Earth. And because money is an innate part of the modern world, one has to interact with this symbol in order to live within it. But that so many people have issues with "money" is an indication of how pervasive root chakra imbalance is and just how much our root chakras need healing.

An imbalanced root chakra also expresses itself as an obsession with the physical body. Extreme compulsions around physical health may actually shroud a deep fear for one's survival. For if someone fears ill health so much that they take obsessive measures to avoid it, it means they are actually focusing not on health but on their fear of death. If someone is overly preoccupied with their youth and beauty, it is because of their fear of aging—a precursor to death. They may also feel that beauty confers a kind of social status that makes it easy to move through the world. Thus, losing their beauty becomes something to obsess over, for they believe it is the only buffer that keeps them from being rejected and cast out of society, without support, unable to survive.

Since food is necessary for physical survival, the root chakra will play a major role in your relationship with it. If, instead of listening to your body, you eat in a way determined by rules created by your mind, you will unbalance your root chakra. Mental rules about food can come as a result of religious beliefs that involve extreme restrictions on what can or cannot be eaten, or on how much food can be eaten at a time. Even well-intended practices like veganism can be an issue if they cause you to ignore your body's unique nutritional needs. Though other chakras have significant roles in eating disorders, they profoundly affect the root chakra because of its relation to the nourishment, and thus survival, of the physical body.

While there are other ways root chakra imbalance can be presented, the above are the ways I have most commonly seen it. Between our ever-mechanized and technological lives and our society's obsession with money, youth, and beauty, grounding is a core issue that needs healing in our lives. This is no coincidence, for the experience of living on Earth is a major part of our spiritual journey, and before we can advance ourselves spiritually we need to understand who we are on a physical level. This means gaining experience and wisdom about the variables inherent to this dimension—which for our bodies means accepting and understanding our primal natures.

When your root chakra is balanced, you accept the physical world for what it is. Instead of fearing its primality, you accept and embrace it. Instead of running away from your physical self, you capitalize on its strengths to enrich your life. You no longer live in a constant state of worry, for when the mind is in tune with your body, it is unable to dominate you. You now have the energy to physically prosper and thrive. You also are now able to receive the energies projected by Mother Earth. Her energy freely passes through the soles of your feet, up your legs, and into the root chakra. But her energy does not stop here—it continues to rise.

As her energy moves upward, each chakra it passes becomes infused with her powerful vibrations. But that's not all. Because the root chakra has now been stabilized, it becomes a strong footing for the chakras above it. The crown chakra can then more widely open to funnel greater amounts of divine energy through it. These energies then move down, and as they pass the other chakras, they become enriched with these vibrations. This energy then moves through the root chakra, down the legs, through the soles of the feet, and into Mother Earth.

This is one of the reasons why we are present in this physical reality, for we are all meant to be vectors to bring spiritual energy from the Universe down to Mother Earth. We help Mother Earth connect to more divine energy by serving as conduits for this energy. This is something Mother Earth could do herself, but as the universal energy moves through us it becomes imbued with our own unique energies and vibrations of love. This is the energy Mother Earth seeks—the energy of her children charged with divine light. For she can then take this energy, filled with our love, connection, appreciation, and honor for her, and reproject it out into the world, healing herself, humanity, and all the other beings that live upon her. This is a process that can happen only if we are grounded. And this is why honoring your root chakra is so important.

How Hematite Can Help

Of all grounding stones, hematite most resonates with the core themes of the root chakra, which is why it is an essential stone for your crystal kit. However, you cannot totally rely on hematite to ground yourself, for no crystal will do all the work for you. In order for you to balance your root chakra, you must integrate other adjunct grounding practices.

Anything that directly connects you to Mother Earth is an activity that will ground you. One way to begin is to place your bare feet onto her. Start communicating with Mother Earth by walking barefoot on soil, grass, sand, or any land that comes directly out of the earth. Anything that puts you in nature like hiking or camping, or anything that has you interacting with the earth, like gardening, will help you as well. Outside of being in nature, the mind-quieting, energy-centering abilities of meditation will always be helpful in grounding yourself. As you engage in practices like these, the scaffolding produced by hematite's energy will help you deeply integrate patterns of grounding that will form an even stronger platform for a balanced root chakra.

Though you can always use hematite for general root chakra support, the following are specific ways hematite can help you with grounding.

TO CALM THE MIND

One of the most frequent questions I get is what stones are helpful for anxiety. While there are deeper, underlying issues that create the sense of anxiety, what always contributes to this feeling is a lack of grounding. When someone feels anxiety, energy is bouncing around inside their head, with each new thought adding further energy that agitates the mind. If this energy has no outlet, it will have nowhere to go except to recycle itself into repetitive thought.

Grounding takes the overabundance of energies from the head and creates an energetic pull downward, allowing the excess energy to move down through the body, into the root chakra, and then down through the legs and feet into Mother Earth. This process creates a pathway for energy to travel, "deflating" the head and allowing energy that was misplaced to be correctly distributed to other chakras as it travels toward the root chakra. If you ground yourself with hematite it will sort out what is happening within your body and thus help illuminate what is causing your anxiety, which helps you get understanding on how you can calm your mind.

TO GROUND ELECTRONIC ENERGIES

Remember in chapter 3 when I said quartz would amplify a computer's electromagnetic frequencies and make it more stressful to work around them (see page 75)? Well, hematite works the opposite way. Hematite is one of the best stones for grounding subtle EMF energies emanating from computers and other electronic equipment. While hematite does not completely negate these energies, it will diminish them.

Botryoidal hematite photographed on my cat, Elvira. Animals are naturally connected with the energy of Mother Earth, so they innately understand—and make exceptional teachers in—grounding. You can learn much from them by observing how present they are within their bodies.

Limonite and hematite pseudomorph after marcasite (aka Prophecy Stone)

Think of hematite as being like energetic earplugs that turn the EMF "volume" lower. Thus hematite is an ideal desktop companion for your computer (it helps to ground all the mental activity around your desk too!).

If you've been thinking a lot, running many different scenarios through your head, it can cause your mind to go into high gear. If you are worried, you may try to push your anxiety away by occupying yourself with other tasks. However, your thoughts will continue to run in the background, keeping your subconscious mind on a mental treadmill. This will cause a surplus of energy to remain in the head. This prevents grounding, which makes sleeping difficult.

Mother Earth is an expert in recycling and transforming energy, for the theme of her body is a constant and simultaneous state of growth, change, and decay. Grounding drains the energy from the mind and directs it into the root chakra; from there any excess energy can be given to Mother Earth, who is then able to take the energy and transmute it for her own benefit.

One of the easiest and most helpful ways to facilitate the movement of overactive mind energy into the ground is by using hematite while sleeping. Placing a tumbled piece of hematite in your pillowcase, or a sizable hunk of it above your head, on your bed stand, or between your legs, can give you the benefits of grounding while you are in your subconscious, sleeping state. For this is a time when your conscious mind is turned off and you are far more open and receptive to any kind of healing that is for your higher good.

As a reminder: All electronics, including phones, should be placed outside the bedroom, or at least across the room. Otherwise, the hematite will divert its energies into grounding the energies of your electronics rather than devoting itself to helping you.

Jet lag is more than a physical experience. In addition to your sleep patterns becoming disrupted, quickly traveling through time zones causes your energetic body to become discombobulated. Like playing a record and then abruptly moving the needle to play another track, your quickly traveling long distances causes a major energetic jog by lifting you from Mother Earth and then touching down somewhere else. The energy of the place you are visiting is different. And not knowing which way the sun rises or sets can disorient you even more. Though some people are hardier when it comes to orienting themselves energetically, for others, flying across many times zones is energetically akin to being stuck in the dryer, tumbled, and then asked to walk straight when they get out.

Since hematite's energy is analogous to the center of the Earth, you can use hematite to help orient yourself energetically. Having a bolder energetic point of grounding helps you to become more easily connected to the land you stand on, shortcutting the energetic adjustment of traveling from one place to another.

TO HELP WITH PERIODS (OR RED BLOOD CELL ISSUES)

The first time I did a crystal grid of hematite around my body, it was before the start of my period, when my desire for consuming iron-rich foods was at its greatest. As I lay with hematite on and around me, I suddenly realized I was smelling the iron coming off of completely polished stones. My body was not only craving iron physically but craving the energetic expression of it as well! Even though the stones had no smell, I so needed hematite's energy that I energetically picked up on its scent.

Hematite is an excellent stone for anyone seeking energetic support with any kind of red blood cell issues. I've had crystal healing clients with anemia who have felt a palpable sense of physical relief when, unbeknownst to them, a hematite-based stone was placed on their body.

Because crystals work on your body on an energetic level, I always tell people with physical ailments to get direct support on the physical level. This can be through medical, nutritional, and other physically based treatments, whether traditional or alternative. But crystals can serve as an adjunct, powerfully helping you on an energetic level to influence your body to heal itself. You may not feel direct physical results from working with the crystals the way you would with strictly physical treatments, but working with crystals can help you discover the emotional, mental, and spiritual pieces contributing to your health issues.

Groundedness is an important theme for those who are dealing with severe illness. If someone has a chance of recovering into a healthy life, hematite is an excellent stone to help them stay oriented in their bodies. By supporting the body's energetic connection to the primal physical experience, hematite activates the root chakra in order to draw on its resources of survival on an energetic level.

But if someone is in hospice or any end-of-life condition, I would discourage the use of hematite. This is because its energy can cause someone who is transitioning out of their physical life to become tied down to their physical body—creating more physical suffering for them. If hematite is intentionally used to keep someone alive in this way, then the act can be a form of black magic that can cause serious karmic repercussions for the person initiating it.

TO CONNECT TO MOTHER EARTH WHEN NOT IN NATURE

There are those who are attracted to cities because they are where they can intellectually thrive. However, by default, the environment of a city can easily cause disconnection from Mother Earth. Thus hematite becomes a very important stone to energetically connect to Mother Earth when you are living in an environment covered in cement and asphalt.

While many noncrystal methods of grounding can be found within the city, such as meditation, walking in a tree-filled park, or feeling a patch of grass under your bare feet, you can still have hematite's energy with you for additional support when you are in places farther removed from Mother Earth's energy. Hematite will heighten your perception of Mother Earth's vibrational energies so that you can stay better connected to her in places that are outside of nature.

TO INCREASE INTUITIVE CAPACITY

Another question I frequently get asked is which stones can help one to become more "psychic." While there are specific stones that encourage psychic ability, opening one's self psychically is a serious problem if you are not grounded.

If you want to open up your psychic abilities or travel to other realities, you want do this without harming yourself. In order to do so, you need to be strongly counterweighted with grounding energy; otherwise opening up to your psychic abilities without the necessary precautions will cause problems you don't want. If you open yourself psychically without being grounded (or protected by a shaman or guide who is holding your energies while guiding you on your inner journey), the surplus of psychic energy will distort your perception long after your initial exposure. The psychic information you receive will be faulty, not grounded in reality, controlled by your mind and its beliefs, and colored by your unfinished business. And these detrimental experiences can lead to anxiety and depression.

You will also be a danger to others. The lack of grounding causes disconnection from physical reality, and this imbalance will cause you to misinterpret other people's energies. What you intuitively "see" and "feel" will be dark, because you will be able to pick up only the portion of energy that matches your own unfinished business. Worse, like a person who has had too much to drink but believes they are still able to drive, the push of psychic energy can trigger your ego, causing you to believe that there are no problems with your perception and that you are in far more psychic control than you are.

You want to be able to increase your psychic sensitivities, but without psychically blowing yourself out and disrupting your own or someone else's life in a detrimental way. The only way to do this is to make sure you are adequately grounded, and hematite is the best stone to teach you how. Hematite helps you connect to your physical body, which helps you connect to yourself and in turn allows you to more clearly see the pieces that are clouding your psychic ability. So if you become grounded, and your heart chakra stays open and tuned in to the perspective of love, it will help you develop your psychic abilities without damage or harm.

TO SUPPORT PROSPERITY

Recall the information from the previous section about grounding and how it relates to physical prosperity. The fundamental requirement for true financial abundance is a strong, healthy relationship to your root chakra. Because hematite resonates with this chakra's core properties, it is the central stone to use for cultivating a deeper connection to the root chakra and the material well-being that can come from it.

As previously stated, the churning of Mother Earth's molten iron outer core against her solid iron center creates the magnetic shield, a "force field" of sorts, that protects our planet from solar winds. In the same way, the energy of iron moving throughout your blood creates an energetic field that helps to contain the boundaries of your energetic space and helps you to deflect any disruptive energies that come from others.

If your "force field" is weak, then other people's energies can encroach on and influence you. You may know someone who makes you feel as if they are always in your personal space even though they don't stand any closer to you than others do. You may also find yourself weirdly influenced by their thoughts and opinions, even though you are conscious of how uncomfortable they make you feel. Or perhaps you have a friend whose only topic of conversation seems to be about their troubles. Because you care for them, you spend time and listen to them, but you find yourself subjected to some variation of the same sob story they have been telling you for years. Even though this friend has plenty of tools and resources, and even though you give them all your help and support, they frustratingly never rise from their problems. You wonder how difficult it could be for someone to improve their lives with everything they have going for them, but this is because you do not realize that you are in a dynamic with someone who is siphoning energy from you.

People like this are unconscious of their behavior, but they are compelled to act in these ways because it gives them an energetic "high." Draining energies from others gives them a boost of energy. Because they do not know how to generate this energy on their own, they search for people whom they can take it from.

Human boundaries are broken by trauma. Whether it's physical, emotional, sexual, or otherwise, the experience of trauma affects one's sense of survival. And because survival is the theme of the root chakra, the root chakra plays a major role in creating your boundaries. While energy cannot be taken from an emotionally healthy person, if you have weaknesses in your root chakra, energy can be taken from you.

You will know if someone you have been with has taken energy from you. Even if you are around them for only a few minutes, the interaction you have with them will make you feel unusually drained and tired. You may also feel an icky heaviness, as though some kind of sticky energetic sludge has been smeared on you. Not only has this person siphoned energy from you, they have energetically slimed you with theirs, leaving you with an unpleasant residue of their interaction to deal with.

But draining energy isn't the only way to infringe on energetic boundaries. Anytime you believe your needs are more important than someone else's, you will push your energy onto them and encroach on their energetic space. This can happen in many small ways. For instance, you may try to get the car in front of you to move faster by driving right behind it, or perhaps you're on the phone with customer service and instead of calmly explaining your situation you dump all your frustrations onto the representative. If in any situation your only concerns are your wants and feelings, you will be pushing your energy onto the person you are interacting with. Even if the interaction is temporary, you are still in a two-way relationship with someone else's energy. The opposite can happen too. If you believe that other people's needs are more important than yours, you will voluntarily allow them to go past your boundaries and come into your energetic space. When you make your needs subservient to others, you give them the right of way to your energy. In order for this not to happen, you must clarify your needs and resolve any limiting beliefs that prevent you from holding your energetic space. Whether you think that you're not special enough to demand respect or that you must martyr yourself and sacrifice your needs in order to be a good person, you alone create the conditions that cause you to be an energetic doormat for others.

Also, be aware that your boundaries are dynamic and can morph and change depending on the situation and who you are interacting with. If you have a mother who constantly sacrifices herself for her kids, putting their needs over her own no matter the circumstance, you have a mother who gives up her boundaries. Though you may not consciously want to take advantage of her, you may find yourself asking for her help even when you don't need it. This is because your mother's energy has set up a dynamic that encourages this to happen. Maybe instead you have a mother

Hematite with rutile

who guilt-trips you into doing things for her. You let her take advantage of you, and thus you allow your mom to encroach on your energetic space. If you don't have solid boundaries, you will be taken advantage of.

The dynamic of boundaries impinging and being impinged upon can even happen with the same person. There may be circumstances where your mother takes advantage of you and other circumstances where you take advantage of her. However, if your goal is spiritual evolvement, it is your job to become aware of both of these dynamics. Though it's the interaction of two people's energies, as the more spiritually aware person you are the one that needs to be more conscientious and disciplined with your energetic space. You are the one who needs to be responsible for your own boundaries and to hold them in such a way that you do not take advantage of others or get taken advantage of.

Boundaries are especially important for empaths and healers because of the way they interact with other people's energies. The psychic ability of an empath will cause them to "feel" others' energies as if these were the energies of their own body. What they will pick up may resonate so closely with some issue already within them that they may unintentionally "accept" another person's energies as if they were their own. If their energetic boundaries are not clear, they will not know how to separate their energies from those of others and will have trouble recognizing what belongs to them and what doesn't. If they do not take care of their boundaries and if they allow their boundaries to become indistinct, they will find themselves infiltrated with other people's energies. Because they feel constantly bombarded, they will avoid social situations and will isolate themselves to avoid dealing with the energies they would otherwise easily absorb.

All healers need to have strong boundaries because the nature of their work means they will interact with energies in a deeper and more complicated way. At this level, energies overlap, making them more challenging to distinguish, so the healer must develop skills that help them recognize the subtleties in different kinds of energy. So in order to facilitate healing for their client, they must delineate the energies being worked on—if these belong to the client, themselves, or even someone or something else. The stronger and clearer a healer's boundaries are, the deeper the healer will be able to go into a client's energies to help heal them. And because all healers have some degree of empathic ability, strong boundaries protect them from mistakenly taking other's people's energy onto themselves. Ultimately, it is a strong energetic boundary that allows the healer to be of greatest service to their clients, for it enables them to distinguish the different energies for what they truly are.

Luckily, we have something quite tactile to model our energies against. Hematite helps you to clarify and strengthen your energetic boundaries. The iron content in hematite makes it a physically heavy stone, so simply holding it can give one a feeling of weight and steadiness. But this sensation also translates on a subtle level, for hematite helps to give your energetic boundaries this same kind of weight and steadiness too.

Hematite asks you to be alert and conscious of your personal space and to be cognizant of any beliefs that would cause you to overstep your bounds or feel that your energy is worth less than that of others. Of all stones, it is the best one to model your energetic boundaries against, for it is the stone that fully embodies the resonance of energetic stability. Hematite will show you how to be disciplined with your energetic space; it will teach you how to keep strong boundaries that allow your energy to flourish, and in turn, allow others the energetic space to flourish as well.

Rose quartz with dendrite inclusion

ROSE QUARTZ

What is the meaning of life?
To love.

There is a lot of confusion about what love is.

Desire, adoration, passion, physical attraction, longing—these emotions are all associated with love, but they aren't love. This is because love is not an emotion. It is in a category of its own.

As souls in pursuit of knowledge, experience, and understanding, we have projected our focus into the physical plane, a new environment in which we could further explore the dynamics of life. We began this journey filled with a great sense of adventure, becoming infatuated with our new playground and everything that could be experienced within it. With a great sense of amusement, we mischievously initiated hijinks just to see what would happen. But our inconsiderate pursuit of fun resulted in many mistakes that caused great pain both to ourselves and to those around us. Because we had purposefully entered a linear environment, we needed to finish the lessons that came with it. Caught in our own setup, we returned lifetime after lifetime to resolve what we began. As we became absorbed with daily life and all its details, our focus became immersed in this reality and we quickly forgot that we are more than just physical beings. But even in our darkest moments as we struggled, even if it was only the smallest, quietest dot of feeling, we never lost the sense that life had some kind of important meaning.

Everything we experience in this world, every lesson we encounter is, at its root, a lesson in love. Love's attributes include compassion, hope, joy, peace, respect, gratitude, understanding, and kindness. In turn, these attributes beget other characteristics including truth, honor, purpose, nurturing, forgiveness, and patience. These subsets would all fall under the grander heading of *love*, the highest vibration in the Universe.

Think about it: The opposite of kindness is cruelty; of respect, contempt; of benevolence, spite. A bully is hurtful, waste is a lack of respect, the person cutting in front of you is inconsiderate, and greed is entitlement that is self-justified. If you follow the thread to the source of any situation containing pain and suffering, you will always find that it was caused by some kind of lack of love. People may believe that they are unhappy because of some issue with their career or finances or relationships and will blame their selected scapegoat in the conviction that it is the reason why they are unhappy and unfulfilled. But if you follow their pain beyond the surface, deeper into the source of the problem, you always find their suffering was caused by a situation needing more love. Because life in the physical plane triggers our fears of scarcity, we convince ourselves that love is in limited supply—that there is not enough to go around and not enough to ever possibly heal us. Yet true love is a divinely infinite, continually generated resource.

Think of someone who was dear to you but has since passed on. Take a moment to remember something about them. As you connect to your memories, recall how they made you feel. Can you feel how much they loved you? Can you also feel how much you loved them? What's so interesting about this exercise is that the love you feel, you are actually feeling *in the present.*

The way things are described in the physical dimension, we use love in the past tense when speaking of someone who is no longer on the physical plane. However, the feeling you experience, both toward the person and from them, is a feeling of love that exists in the present. Though you may have initially felt grief and sadness, what persists and outlasts all other feelings is not a memory of this feeling but the feeling of love, *now.* This is because the vibration of love never degrades. Once the connection is created, it remains in infinity, even when you are not sensing it.

You may have not realized this, but you have always had the ability to create unlimited amounts of love. No matter how much love you have created and put into the world, you are still able to make more. You don't have a limited amount to parcel to a certain number of people. Nor do you need to take love away from someone in order to give it to someone else. You are able to generate love with no loss to anyone, including yourself. In fact, the more you generate, the more love you feel. Though you are a single, humble human being, you have been born endowed with the power to perpetually generate the highest vibration in the Universe. So why is it so difficult to do so?

Rose quartz geode (left) and pink quartz (right)

Because you are still in the process of learning about love.

As a soul, you came to the physical plane to learn about both sides of an experience. You were going to experience hurting others and then learn what it felt like to be hurt. In these lessons, you were abandoned and traumatized, and because of the pain that you felt, you could not feel the love that was always there. As you continued through your lifetimes, as you mastered each spiritual lesson of love, you dissolved the enemies you had self-created in fear. Whittling down your list, you eliminated many illusory foes until you met the greatest and worst enemy of all—yourself. Though you had come very far, learning to love the world and others, you still had to fully learn the greatest lesson on the physical plane, *how to love yourself.* For how you treat the world is a reflection of how you treat yourself. To become more loving of the world means looking closely at yourself, seeing what you don't accept about who you are, and then learning to accept and love yourself. And this has been the most challenging lesson of your spiritual journey.

Love is an overarching experience, a context that holds all emotions. This is why you can be angry at someone, hurt by them, or disappointed in them, yet love them just the same. Love does not change because of emotions. It is a constant, a force that holds the energy of all creation.

Everyone in the physical dimension is learning how to embody love, but at different levels of mastery. Some are young souls who are just beginning to gather the experiences of life. Others are old souls who have been around many times before and have a better understanding of love's purpose. But if you can step back and look at the world without judgment, you will see that everyone has been doing the best they can to learn their lessons about love.

The lesson of love is an infinite one with ever-deepening levels to understand at each step of your journey. Love is the only thing that heals the wounds of the soul. It heals fear, guilt, and shame and brings people closer together. Love opens the heart and brings compassion, peace, kindness, and healing. There is nothing greater than love. *Love* is the meaning of life. It is the purpose of why we are here.

Above all, rose quartz is the stone that resonates with the core purpose of universal love. Unlike other stones, its energy is not overt and dynamic but rather has a gentle and steady quality to its vibration. The energy it emanates can be likened to a warm hug from a loving mother to her child; the gentle, happy wag of a dog's tail; the soothing vibration from the contented purring of a cat on your lap.

Rose quartz energy is so soft and present that it can seem vibrationally still. But this is almost a trick, for its unassuming vibration belies a most powerful strength. For what rose quartz does is pull you into your own energy, closer to the center of yourself, so that it may gently present the pieces within you needing more healing and love. As you go deeper into your layers, resolving even deeper wounds, it brings you closer to the center of your heart. And it is here in your heart where the greatest power within you lies—the ability to generate and manifest unlimited quantities of the omnipotent vibration of love to give to yourself and the world.

When you have reached a certain point of understanding, you will truly realize how powerful love is and how a simple change in your vibration of it can create a "butterfly effect" that affects the whole of the Universe. Not only does rose quartz help you to fundamentally understand this, but it can help you recognize and feel these effects too. Quieting yourself and meditating with rose quartz can help you to feel how the center of your heart is the center of the Universe—for the center of your heart is *love!*

This understanding of your own God-nature increases as you venture deeper into the spiritual core within your heart. Because there is always another layer to discover, another deeper layer to understand, the journey of your soul becomes infinite with no final destination except toward even deeper love. This is the true spiritual ecstasy you have been searching for and are in the process of discovering. And it is what rose quartz is here to help you connect to.

When to Use Rose Quartz

Because the lesson of rose quartz is so encompassing, it can be broadly used in *any situation* where more love is needed.

- If you're having a bad day (or could just use a hug)

- If you're having a great day (or want to enhance any feelings of love and happiness)

Found in rough chunks, this kind of rose quartz is
relatively plain and humble. But its modesty belies
one of the most powerful stones in crystal healing.

- When you want to bring more love into a place, situation, or person (including yourself)

- Any time you want to more deeply connect to the resonance of love, or any of its attributes (e.g., acceptance, forgiveness, understanding, kindness)

Remember, the vibration of rose quartz is of a universal, unconditional love—and this is the core of our soul's journey. As you can always go deeper into this lesson, it is a stone to be used liberally.

Types of Rose Quartz

Though there are other varieties of pink-hued quartz, the most important benefits of rose quartz are present in its most modest and inexpensive form—as plain, humble chunks of semitranslucent pink rock.

From this rough form, rose quartz can be polished into different shapes like spheres, oval gallets, or cabochons for jewelry. But the way you will most likely encounter rose quartz is as tumbled stones small enough to be slipped into your pocket. Since love is what you need the most, you want to use rose quartz generously in your life. I recommend having one sizable piece, something that would fit in your palm or hand, to work closely with. Working with tumbled stones or other easily transportable forms of rose quartz will always be useful for you too, for it will keep you working consistently with rose quartz energy.

A Question about Your Life

Write down one question about your life you want insight on.

Make sure it's *one question* about *one specific topic*. Asking "Is taking this new job and getting serious about the person I'm dating the right change for my life?" actually covers two different topics and may have two different answers.

Instead, you'll want to phrase the question so that you are asking specifically about the job or about the person you're dating. Otherwise you will get a blended answer that covers two topics at the same time. The results will be muddy and will make your answer unclear.

Additionally, you will want to avoid vague questions, which will lead to vague answers. Instead, be specific. "How can I improve my life?" is a broad question. Asking "How can I improve my life emotionally?" or even more specifically, "How can I improve my life romantically?" will allow you to receive clearer, more precise answers.

Write this question in your notebook and go on to read the next chapters. It will be helpful to take a break and to focus on other things before you get your answer.

Rainbow lattice

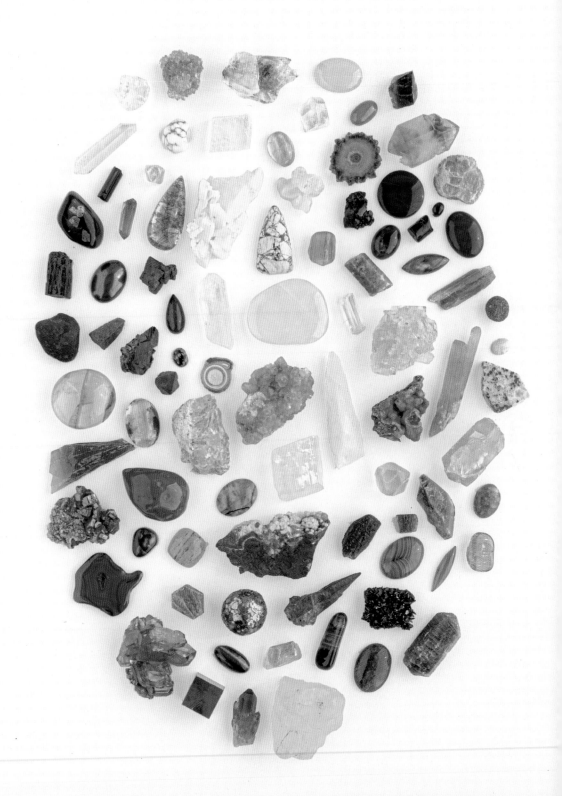

CHAPTER 5

CRYSTALS, COLORS, AND CHAKRAS

BEFORE I BECAME A CRYSTAL HEALER, I always wondered how authors of crystal books knew how a crystal related to a particular chakra. Was it some special gift? It seemed as though these authors belonged to some elite metaphysical club whose crystal secrets were revealed only to the most psychically gifted. Perhaps I needed decades, even lifetimes, of metaphysical training before I could get even a glimpse of the understanding that these crystal savants had. But when I went to study under my crystal teacher, Katrina Raphaell, founder of the Crystal Academy of Advanced Healing Arts, I discovered that the relationship between crystals and chakras was easy enough for anyone, even someone with zero metaphysical training, to understand. But before you learn how simple it is, you must first have an understanding of what chakras *are*.

In the last chapter, I explained how the root chakra manages grounding energy for you (see page 104). But you have additional chakras that manage other energies for you too. Derived from Sanskrit, meaning "wheels of light," *chakras* are metaphysical portals located in your subtle body that extend outward in the front and back of your body. And just as a prism separates white light into different colors of the rainbow, chakras distribute your metaphysical energy into different categories. Like spinning tops, these chakras emanate revolving vortexes that separate, collect, and transmit metaphysical energy.

While you have thousands of chakras emanating from your subtle body, the most significant ones run along the length of your spine, from the base of your tailbone to the top of your head. The number of these major chakras, as well as their exact location and purpose, depends on the system. The Tibetan, Cherokee, Mayan, Incan, ancient Egyptian, and Zulu cultures, as well as the energetic systems of Kabbalah and Chinese chi, all have their own variation on the energy portal system (though there are similarities that are significant). Common to many of the different systems are individual chakras that manage your energetic relationship to your physical body and to your survival, emotions, love, communication, thinking, and connection to the divine. Of all the systems, the most familiar and widely accepted in modern Western culture is based on the Vedic system of seven major chakras. If you've gone into a yoga studio or metaphysical shop and seen a rainbow banner with a different symbol within each of the seven colors, this is the system that is being illustrated.

Each of your chakras rotates with energy, but the quality of motion they exhibit is dependent on their state. Your chakras can be in a state of overrotation (too much energy), underrotation (not enough energy), or balance (just right). Because individually your chakras can be in any one of these possible states, you can have a combination of balanced, overactivated, and underactivated chakras all at the same time. But these states are not static; they are always in flux, shifting from one state to another depending on how they respond to energy as it moves through them.

This means that whatever combination of states your chakras are in can be shifted by any new inflow of energy. Perhaps you are getting frustrated (energy that is being produced from within you), or someone is angry with you (energy that is coming from outside of you that you are likely pulling into yourself). The more balanced your individual chakras are, the more likely it is that you will be able to process this energy and bounce back to a balanced state. But any over- or underrotating chakras are likely to be pushed farther in their respective direction of unbalance. There will be some situations (like spilling food on a new shirt) that may trigger only small flare-ups of passing emotion and experience, while other situations (like a bad breakup) cause a more persistent effect on your chakras because of the amount and depth of energy needed to process and move through the experiences.

Balancing and strengthening your chakras will improve their resiliency. Even improving the resiliency of just one chakra can help all your chakras as a whole. This is because a single balanced chakra can act as a stabilizer, giving the other unbalanced chakras a point of reference to orient themselves to. And the more balanced a chakra is, the more even and consistent its spin is, making it far less prone to being knocked out of place by any other force of energy, whether it is generated from outside or inside of yourself.

The more balanced your chakras become, the more balanced the energies you will project into your aura—and the more balanced the energy is that you send out into the world. Though balancing your chakras may seem an insignificant deed compared to fixing the larger problems of the world, by doing so you will have actually made a significant contribution to the world's healing. For not only will you have created more peace, love, and harmony for yourself, you will also project the neutral energies of peace, love, and harmony for the world to interact with; this is because the energy you express will lack the polarity that would incite others to be pulled out of balance when interacting with you.

THE CHAKRAS AND CRYSTALS

Because chakras work within a specific focus of energy, they also have a specific range of frequency. This causes them to resonate with anything that has the same frequency of vibration. Thus chakras can have parallel affinities to astrological signs, symbols, numbers, planets, musical notes, foods, and more. In the previous chapter, I went into detail about why hematite's energy most strongly parallels the qualities of the root chakra (see page 106). While hematite is the crystal most resonant with the root chakra's purpose, a great many other crystals also resonate with root chakra energy. How to determine this, or what other crystals go with what chakra, is quite simple— all you need to learn is the relationship between *chakras* and *color*.

As I mentioned above, the chakra colors of the Vedic system mirror the bands of color found on a rainbow. Beginning with the root chakra and the color red, the colors progress through the rainbow with each chakra until you reach the crown chakra and the color violet. While the seven-chakra Vedic system is ideally suited for a broad range of energetic healing applications like Reiki and color therapy, because crystals have been created in the density of the physical plane, they have a range and distribution of coloring that is more dense than the pure color energies represented in the Vedic system. Thus the following eight-chakra system, as taught to me by Katrina Raphaell, has proven to be both a simple and powerful system to work with in conjunction with crystals, for it most strongly reflects how crystalline energy has been distributed on the physical plane and, in my experience as a crystal healer, works exceedingly well for the range and distribution of colors that crystals come in. All you need do to apply it is to **match the color of the stone with the color of the chakra**!

As you'll see in the chart on the next page, each of the eight major chakras correspond to a specific color, which can then be matched to the color of the stone or crystal you are working with. While the crystal will have its metaphysical properties influenced by its chemical makeup and crystalline lattice, the crystal's color will determine which chakra it most resonates with. Even if you were colorblind and could not see the crystal's actual color, the crystal would still affect the chakra with which it resonates, because the wavelength at which the color vibrates would not change.

Though there are rare exceptions of stones that will resonate more strongly with chakras other than the chakra color they match, it's not something to concern yourself with. Although crystals do have affinities to certain chakras, this does not mean that a crystal's energy will be limited to just one chakra. In fact, there are many instances where using a crystal for a different chakra is quite beneficial. Because your unique energies interact with a crystal in an individual way, you may benefit from what is considered a "nontraditional" pairing of crystal to chakra. Remember: Crystals are very much like food. Pairings like avocado ice cream or tomato cake may be unusual for many, but as long as these foods taste good to you, that's all that counts. Likewise, as long as you get helpful results from a crystal's energy, that is all that matters. And experimenting with a crystal on different chakras deepens your intuitive connection with the crystal itself, allowing you to develop a better, more well-rounded understanding of how the crystal is personally able to help you.

You will also encounter stones that are a mixture of the main chakra colors. For instance, prehnite is often chartreuse, a mixture of yellow and green. Because the green color resonates with the solar plexus and the yellow with the navel chakra, this crystal can be used on either chakra, or in between the two chakras. Orange stones, like an orange-colored calcite or spessartine garnet, resonate with both the yellow navel chakra and the red creative chakra, or in between.

THE EIGHT-CHAKRA SYSTEM FOR CRYSTALS

CHAKRA	COLOR	LOCATION	EXAMPLE STONES
Crown	Colorless/ white	Center of the top of the head	Clear quartz, selenite, phenakite
Third eye	Purple/ indigo	Between the eyes	Amethyst, purpurite, sodalite, lapis
Throat	Light blue	Base of the neck, where the clavicles meet	Blue lace agate, angelite, blue barite
Heart	Pink	Between the nipples in the center of the chest	Rose quartz, pink calcite, rhodochrosite
Solar plexus	Green	Beneath the ribs under the sternum	Malachite, green aventurine, jade
Navel	Yellow	Umbilical point	Tiger's eye, citrine, pyrite
Creative	Red	Halfway between the navel and the pubic bone	Vanadinite, crocoite, red garnet
Root	Black	Center of the bottom of the pubic bone at the base of the spine	Smoky quartz, black tourmaline, hematite

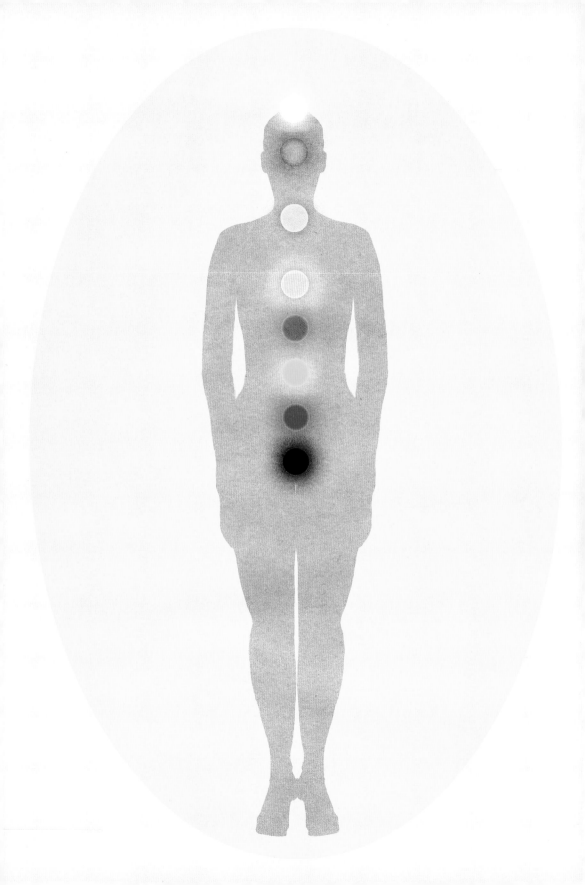

Labradorite is an example of a stone that changes color depending on what direction you look at it from. This effect is the result of an optical phenomenon called chatoyancy that causes the concentration of reflected light to change as the mineral is turned.

Some crystals clearly exhibit bands of different colors within the same stone. For instance, the crystal ametrine is a hybrid of amethyst and citrine quartz and contains distinct purple and golden yellow zones of color. In this case, the crystal resonates both with the purple of the third eye chakra and the yellow of the navel chakra and can be used with either. Watermelon tourmaline, like its namesake, has distinct sections of pink and green that resonate with the heart and solar plexus chakras. These are examples of dual-purpose stones, which have relationships with more than one chakra and serve a special purpose linking up the energies between them. They also help reveal the relationships between the different chakras and how they are able to work together to bring healing to each respective area.

Sometimes you will encounter a stone like labradorite that generally reads as deep blue while also having flashes of red, yellow, and green, depending on the way the stone is refracting the light. Though you see all the other colors, the dark blue is the most predominant, making the stone most resonant with the third eye chakra.

You may also encounter stones that do not have a color that can be easily matched with a chakra. These stones tend not to be bold in color and are far more drab in hue. Perhaps the crystal in question is somewhat red, or maybe a little orangey red—or maybe brown? You can't quite decide. That's okay. The best thing to do is to go with the first impression you have of the stone's color. If red was your first response, try using it with your creative chakra. Otherwise, try using it with another chakra and test it out to see how the crystal works with you.

Going with your first response is a technique that is also helpful for stones that contain a multitude of colors, like many kinds of agates and jaspers. For instance, blue lace agate is a stone with bands of light blue and white, but when you look at it, the overall impression of color is of light blue. A stone like rainforest jasper has patches of yellow, orange, and whitish gray, but the dominant color that you see is green. So whenever you have a stone that has many various colors but one overarching dominant color, the dominant color would be the main color to choose to pair with a chakra. And another note: Even if someone else looks at the same stone and has a different opinion of the stone's color, remember the stone is interacting with **your** energies. Thus the color you see is the color that is going to be most helpful to you.

Ametrine is a combination of natural
amethyst and citrine found in the
same crystal. Because it has both
amethyst and citrine energies, it will
simultaneously resonate with both the
third eye and navel chakras.

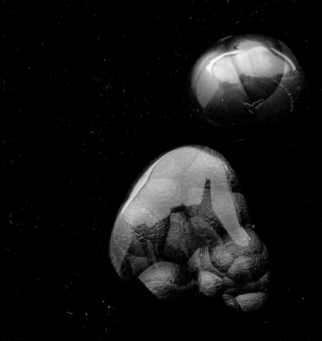

Because fire agates predominantly exhibit
the color red, they resonate most strongly
with the creative chakra. But because they
also display iridescence, each will also
resonate with any chakras it shows colors for.

You may even see the same kind (aka species) of stone expressed in different colors. This is because specific conditions in Mother Earth will change the color of the crystal while it is growing. For instance, calcite from one location may be white while in another part of the world it's blue. You may even find different hues within the same mineral vein; this happens because there are ultraspecific conditions, different trace minerals as well as potentially a different microclimate, that affect the final shape and color of a stone. It is the final color that is expressed, the color that you see, that you refer to in order to determine which chakra the crystal best resonates with.

If you already have a collection of crystals, this is a good moment to observe the palette of colors you have. If you notice that your collection gravitates toward a specific color, it could mean that you have needed to work with the particular chakra that the color is associated with. But if you significantly lack any other colors of stones, it's likely to mean that the chakra whose color you have been most attracted to is overactivated. Focusing on one particular chakra means you are giving it attention and energy at the expense of the others. This lopsided dispersal of attention is detrimental to your overall healing, because it means you have been ignoring the needs of your other chakras in favor of one chakra. The chakra will be overactivated and will pull energies from the other chakras in order to maintain its overactive state, putting the rest of your chakras in a state of imbalance.

Remember, all healing is about balance. This also applies to healing yourself through the crystals with a balance of colors. So as you continue to add crystals to your tool kit, be cognizant of having a balance of crystals that will be supportive with all your chakras.

Now you are no longer in mystery and have the information to determine which crystal goes with what chakra! See how simple it was to pair them?

Each one of these crystals is a form of calcite—and
each resonates with a different chakra based on
their most dominant color.

Slices of naturally multicolored tourmalines

THE EIGHT-CHAKRA SYSTEM

In order to get the most out of crystalline healing energy, it's important to have an understanding of the major chakras and the role each plays in your spiritual health. It is a subject worthy of more in-depth study than will be covered by this book; in the meantime, the following summaries will help orient you to the purposes of the different chakras so that you can understand how each influences you.

This eight-chakra system, taught to me by my crystal teacher, Katrina Raphaell, is a system that I have found works very synergistically with crystalline energy. As you continue with your studies, the relationship between chakras and crystals will become more significant, and this information will help you better understand your own healing process as well as the energetic potential within each crystal you encounter.

ROOT CHAKRA

Theme	Survival
Purpose	To show that you are fully supported by Mother Earth and have everything you need to thrive on her; to connect and ground higher divine energies through the physical body and then into Mother Earth.
When Balanced	Security and vitality with physical health and wealth. Nonjudgment of physicality and its primal, animal nature. Connected to Earth and its energies and patterns. Clear and balanced energetic boundaries.
When Overactive	Material desperation, greed, fear of nature, obsessive sexuality bereft of love or soul-fulfilling pleasure; preoccupation with illness, being physically harmed, death, and/or dying; ungrounded from being unbalanced by too much psychic or mental activity.
When Underactive	Apathy to survival, a life of extreme control or predictability, denial of one's animal nature, poverty consciousness, physical laziness.

CREATIVE CHAKRA

Theme	Vitality
Purpose	To show that physical life is also physical pleasure; that this is healthy as long as it is in balance with the rest of your life. To practice sex in a higher, more sacred form. To express the playfulness within sensate experiences that are the precursors to creativity.
When Balanced	A healthy and pleasurable relationship with food, sex, smells, physical movement, rest, and other physically based sensations. Sensuality and sex as an expression of love and intimacy. Vitality and zest for physical life.
When Overactive	Lust, gluttony, hedonism, lack of moderation, the perceived need for drugs and alcohol in order to have "fun" in one's life.
When Underactive	Sloth, indifference, or overly strict denial of sensuality.

NAVEL CHAKRA

Theme	Manifestation
Purpose	To bring the conceptual into physical manifestation. To assimilate and process experiences in order to fully understand all the factors that contribute to manifestation. To learn lessons about personal power.
When Balanced	Ability to transition the energy of ethereal thoughts and ideas into tangible physical reality. Being in charge of one's life. Balanced use of willpower. The sense of empowerment.
When Overactive	Desperation or the brute use of force to achieve goals. Overconfidence. Goals manifested in a corrupted form.
When Underactive	Lethargy or apathy toward manifestation in one's life. Inability to manifest. The perception that one lacks power.

SOLAR PLEXUS CHAKRA

Theme	Emotions
Purpose	To teach you the importance of feelings. To use them as an essential way of understanding yourself and your truth. To use emotions in a just, fair, and compassionate way toward yourself and others. To show how emotions and feelings are a direct connection to intuitive information.
When Balanced	Healthy expression of all emotions. The expression of feelings at the right moment in balanced ways. Being true to oneself emotionally.
When Overactive	Emotions used to inflict pain or control on others. Lack of awareness with one's emotions. Impinging on others' emotional spaces.
When Underactive	Denial, resistance, repression, and/or avoidance of feelings. Ennui.

HEART CHAKRA

Theme	Love
Purpose	To embody the highest and most powerful vibration in the Universe, love. To express and project this love and its subsets into the world. To serve as an energetic bridge translating information between the lower physical chakras (root chakra to solar plexus) and the upper spiritual chakras (heart to crown). To teach how love for the world is synonymous with love of self. Universe. To understand that love is what underlies all things.
When Balanced	Based and centered on love. Innate joyfulness. Peacefulness with others and the world. Self-love. Acceptance of self and others.
When Overactive	The need to rescue others. Placing others before one's self. Excessive desire to please. Martyrdom.
When Underactive	Sadness, loneliness, emptiness, despondence. Feelings of shame.

THROAT CHAKRA

Theme	Communication
Purpose	To express your unique talents and your highest truth. To understand the importance of the energy behind words, and using them with intention. To say what you mean and mean what you say. The lesson of listening.
When Balanced	Unhindered expression of one's self. Ability to openly and freely express one's thoughts and feelings. The ability to listen clearly. Integrity of words and thus action.
When Overactive	Talking over people. Domineering in communication. Inability to listen to others. Garrulousness.
When Underactive	Extreme shyness or quietness. Avoidant communication especially with difficult subjects. Denying expression of one's true self and talents.

THIRD EYE CHAKRA

Theme	Inner sight
Purpose	To develop and refine intuitive ability. To perceive the differences between psychic impression, imagination, projection, fantasy, and illusion. To develop perceptive clarity. To be able to direct the mind rather than be led by it.
When Balanced	Ability to discern between thoughts, emotions, and psychic impressions from mental thought. Psychic abilities grounded into reality.
When Overactive	Anxious and/or obsessive thinking. Worry. Inaccurate psychic impressions. Distorted spirituality. Strict reliance on intelligence.
When Underactive	Lack of imagination. Lack of connection to one's psychic abilities.

CROWN CHAKRA

Theme	Oneness
Purpose	To realize one's connection to divinity. To understand that one is connected to the greater whole of life and the Universe. To embody knowingness. To be a channel for divine energy to come through one's self. To develop wisdom. To experience enlightenment and bliss.
When Balanced	Trusting. Tranquil. In a state of inner knowing.
When Overactive	Paranoia. Egoism.
When Underactive	Mistrust. Suspicion.

Examples of in-between colored stones.
Clockwise from top: astrophyllite, calcite,
coprolite, spinel in marble, and wavellite

Balancing Chakras

Your chakras are dynamic, always processing energy, and thus always in a state of flux. But each of your chakras has a "default setting" that you have established by habitually dealing with life's situations in a particular way. This creates an energetic set point for each chakra, and from it, its "normal" range of expression. What some chakras consider "normal" may actually be unhealthily skewed, but as you continue to strengthen them, your set points for them will gradually move toward a healthier and more balanced state.

It's important to remember that bringing chakras into greater balance is not a linear process, for each of your individual chakras is at a different stage of healing. Although the balancing of a single chakra can significantly contribute to the stability and balance of other chakras, it is not unusual for a newly balanced chakra to throw off other, formerly balanced chakras. When you straighten a pipe bent at many angles, one evened-out kink can cause the entire pipe to bend a different way. This sort of ripple effect also happens when a newly balanced chakra, whose energy now flows without impedance, influences how energy flows throughout the chakra system on the whole. The once-stable chakras now waver, revealing the compensatory energetic architecture that was created to keep energy moving through the system. Fortunately, because they are already familiar with the "tone" of a more balanced state, chakras will have an easier time finding their way back to balance.

It is also important to understand that "chakra balance" does not mean a static state of perfection but rather a state of being. Because you are constantly challenged by the interactions you have with yourself and the world, your chakras will always experience an ebb and flow of energy. And like a dancer who must shift their balance every time they change position, your chakras are also in an active state, keeping themselves in balance with any new energies they encounter. This means there will be situations that you will have an easier time staying in balance with, while other scenarios you will find to be more difficult. For example, your heart chakra may find it easy to freely give and receive love from animals but may find it much harder to do the same with people. Or perhaps you generally have a great deal of patience and kindness for humankind but have a certain relative who grates on your nerves in the worst possible way. So while on the whole your heart chakra may be in balance, there are still circumstances and situations that will challenge its ability to stay centered. Thus the state of being in balance with your chakras is an ongoing process.

However, each new experience you have will show you where you can become more skilled at maintaining balance, teaching you to become more perceptive to the nuances of energy within each of your chakras as you learn to recognize their individual tendencies. This results in each encounter becoming yet a deeper lesson in the understanding and practice of chakra balance. Like an acrobat who is able to balance on top of a unicycle while on a tightrope, you will develop more precision with your balance, as well as greater strength to regain it, so that situations you once found difficult you will no longer find challenging.

"Love is not love which alters
when it alteration finds."
—William Shakespeare, "Sonnet 116"

OPPOSITE: True citrine comes in a range of colors, from pale yellow to dark amber to a yellowish-tinged smoky gray-brown. As seen here, even citrine rods from the same locality come in different yellows; variations occur even within a crystal itself.

ABOVE: Sometime during this quartz's growth, it became dusted with a layer of hematite. The quartz continued to grow on top of it, leaving an outline or "phantom" of hematite.

Crystal spheres. This page, top to bottom:
black tourmaline with chrysocolla, blue lace
agate, rose quartz. Opposite, top to bottom:
ocean jasper, lepidolite, quartz, pinolith

"Love is metaphysical gravity."
—Buckminster Fuller

"Who knows whether this tumult
of triangles inscribed in stone, first
brought about by nature and then
by art, does not contain one of the
secret cyphers of the universe?"
—Roger Caillois,
The Writing of Stones

OPPOSITE: Natural triangle-shaped etchings
on the surface of a quartz crystal

ABOVE: Quartz with a naturally sharp point

CHAPTER 6

HOW TO RECOGNIZE AND WHY TO AVOID ARTIFICIALLY ENHANCED CRYSTALS

UNFORTUNATELY, the popularity of metaphysical crystals has created a hot market for fake crystals. By nature, metaphysics depends on personal experience, and because of this no verification agency for metaphysical crystals can ever exist. Consequently, because consumers do not realize the prevalence of fake crystals on the market, they become easy marks for sellers of dubious stones with purported metaphysical properties. While some sellers of fake crystals sincerely believe they are providing customers with supportive metaphysical crystals, others are looking for a way to turn a profit and find metaphysical buyers a gullible target.

What follows is an overview of crystals that have been artificially treated to their detriment, covering the spectrum from merely sad to very messed up. I'll explain what has been done to them, how to spot it, and how these treatments metaphysically affect the crystals. By the end of this chapter, you'll be far more aware of the differences between truly resonant metaphysical crystals and their imposters.

POLISHED QUARTZ POINTS

In chapter 3, I talked about how quartz is built from silicon dioxide molecules stacked in parallel spirals that conjoin into a single point (see page 73). But quartz points don't always come out of the ground with their tips sharp and clear. Instead, they can often be found naturally coated in other minerals that obscure or cloud their transparency. Sometimes these coatings can be removed without damaging the crystal underneath, but in many cases this is not possible. Consumers, not understanding the value of natural quartz points and believing translucent crystals to be "prettier" or more powerful than the coated versions, reject buying points in their natural, unadulterated form. In response to this demand for more "attractive" crystals, many quartz miners trim and grind the crystals to make them more appealing for sale. While the transparency of the crystal is enhanced, it is at the expense of the metaphysical power of the crystal, for the magical, turbo-boosting spirals, which before had harnessed the powerful energy moving through the crystal and coalesced this energy into a precise, directional tip, have now been chopped off. Also forever destroyed are the specialized gateways of metaphysical information found only through growth ridges and other natural etchings on the crystal's surface, which have now been razed in the attempt to make the quartz more physically appealing and saleable.

It takes a lot of care to make sure a crystal comes out of the ground fully intact, without chips and dings to the crystal. But many miners, not wanting to be bothered with meticulousness, hastily dig up crystals in such a way that they get dinged up, tossed around, and damaged. They find it far easier to polish the points afterward, and anyhow, the altered crystals still put money in their pocket.

Businesses specializing in altered crystal points can be so adept at cutting and polishing that their cuts will still align with the original points of the crystal. Because of these skills, one can be easily fooled into believing their crystal has been unaltered, especially if the crystal point doesn't have telltale clues like misaligned phantoms (see page 170). But the biggest giveaway can be found at the base of the crystal: If the base is flat, often with a beveled edge, the crystal has been artificially polished. Another clue can be found on the surface of the crystal faces. If the crystal lacks any natural surface etchings or growth ridges, this is likely to signify that its surfaces have been ground off. Also in many instances the natural etchings on the sides of the crystal have been left intact, but the faces where the crystal meets at the tip have been artificially ground to a point. You will find this particular treatment across the board, from large "decorator-size" crystals to points thinner than the width of your finger. You'll even find this treatment on crystal clusters where multiple tips have been polished in such a way as to make it appear as though the cluster has always been in perfect, unmarred condition. Often this work can be quite subtle, but you can learn to determine if polishing has happened with careful observation. If you inspect

Artificially polished quartz point, with a beveled bottom and misaligned phantoms. This is the crystalline equivalent of clipping the tip of a leaf because it's not "perfect" enough.

Notice the different textures on the faces of this quartz crystal. While some faces have a completely smooth surface or striated bands caused by the crystal's growth, the largest face has a satiny quality to it. This is because this face has been artificially ground down to remove the chips and dings that would make it less "pretty" and thus less saleable.

these crystals closely, you will notice that the polished surfaces are visually and texturally more satiny, while the rest of the crystal looks and feels relatively more glassy. You will also notice that edges of the polished surfaces are ever so slightly rounded instead of being clean and sharp. With practice, you will be able to determine if a treatment has happened simply by running a finger along an edge of the crystal to feel if it's sharp or vaguely curved.

But before you reject and grieve over any polished quartz points you have in your collection, know the situation is salvageable. Though modified quartz is not ideal, it is still a powerful stone that will continue to work for programming, turbo-boosting, and other energetic quartz magic—just not as purely and directly as an unadulterated point can. Even though the crystal has been altered, what will ultimately give the most power to your stone is your attention and understanding.

For instance, my spiritual mentor has an incredibly powerful crystal point—one of the most vibrant I have ever seen. Even though it has been cut and polished, it is alive and full of potent energy. This is because she knows how to interact with this crystal by recognizing its abilities, giving it attention, and working with the stone with intention. Like a good friend who "gets you" and whose understanding makes you blossom when they are near, my mentor's stone resonates with power because it is infused by the energy of someone who understands its abilities. This is why skeptical people have no metaphysical experiences with crystals—because you have to consciously engage with a crystal in order to activate its energies. Otherwise, nothing happens. So if you know how to work with crystals, you can make even an impaired crystal resonate with powerful, healing intensity.

OTHER POLISHED AND CUT STONES

"But what about gemstones and other polished stones?" people ask me. "Is it bad for them that they are cut and polished too?"

"The answer," I say, "has to do with *intention*."

Many rocks come out of the ground looking like—well, rocks. They often look dull and boring, seeming to lack any special attributes. But when they are cut and polished, patterns and colors once hidden in their roughness begin to appear, revealing the stones' beauty. This intensifies your visual connection to the stones, which increases your appreciation of their beauty, and the deeper emotional link created allows you to be better connected to the stones' energy. This same principle also applies to gemstones, which are cut and polished from more costly semiprecious and precious geological material.

Gemstones can look pretty underwhelming in their raw, unpolished form, often looking like dull-colored pieces of half-eaten hard candy. But when they are expertly faceted, light is able to enter and refract within the stones, enhancing their sparkle and/or color. Then, when a stone is lovingly cut, it becomes more energetically vibrant. The respect, honor, thought, and attention that have gone into cutting the stone are what helps to reveal the stone's hidden beauty, which in turn allows you to better connect with the gemstone's metaphysical energy. But sadly, most gemstones lack this kind of intention.

For most of my life, gemstones did nothing for me. Even when looking at the finest jewelry stores on Rodeo Drive, I found them unimpressive, but I couldn't quite put my finger on why. Then one day I was introduced to the work of a lone custom gemstone cutter whose work was so exquisite that it made me want to do backflips. Never in my life had I seen gemstones so mesmerizing, and as I got to know his work I began to understand what made his stones so different. Instead of mindlessly whittling down a rough gemstone to fit some traditional shape, he would examine a stone over and over again until he fully understood how to bring out its ultimate beauty. He carefully considered how to cut the stone so the light moving through it would enhance its color while only carving away the barest amount of material that kept the beauty of the stone hidden from human eyes. In every step of the process, he gave the stone in front of him his full attention and his wholehearted care, with the intention to coax the most beauty he could out of every stone— and it showed.

This is why intention is so important when cutting crystals and stones: One must be clear about why a stone would benefit from being cut rather than being left in a raw state. One must also understand how a treatment will affect the crystal's energy. And one must know the kind of cutting the stone itself would benefit from. Otherwise, one will be mindlessly harming the stone.

For instance, the iconic shape of quartz has led other minerals to be ground into artificial points that mirror its six-sided shape. The most common example of this is with fluorite, which is often shaped to look like a quartz point. But this is actually a dishonor to fluorite's energy because, unlike quartz, it is built from molecules that stack themselves into cubes or octahedrons. In comparison, as explained in chapter 3, quartz is built from tetrahedral molecules, shaped like little pyramids, which naturally stack on top of each other in spirals to ultimately create a six-sided shape (see page 73). While this shape is ideally suited for supporting quartz's turbo-boosting powers, it is in contradiction to fluorite's energy, which is about steadiness. The energetic clashing produced from the interaction between fluorite's natural energy and its imposed shape diminishes fluorite's overall power and prevents it from fully projecting its healing energies. It is exactly this kind of carelessness that makes crystals sad, for it prevents them from freely expressing their energy in the most healing and supportive way. But it is the kind of carelessness that keeps happening because it makes money for somebody.

crystals at very high heat for half a day, they become an orangey-yellow approximation of citrine that feeds the hungry citrine market.

Although heat-treated citrines still resonate with manifestation energy, they do so at a cost. Because natural citrines develop their color through the slow and patient craftsmanship of Mother Earth, the manifestation energy they resonate

Artificial citrine, identifiable by its burnt-orange color

with is gentle but productive. But like the wan results of hastily microwaved food, the quick process used to create heat-treated citrines causes them to have a loud and garish energy. Much like a person who barks at a store employee and gets her demands met just because the employee wants her to go away, heat-treated citrines manifest with a pushy energy that imposes on others rather than nurtures outcomes that are soul-satisfying for everyone involved. Though heat-treated citrine can get you results, it's not the kind of energy you want for manifestation. Instead, it is better to wait and find a true piece of natural citrine or to use a different kind of manifestation stone—which will be more powerful than a stone like heat-treated citrine that has been forced to be something that it is not.

If you already have a heat-treated citrine, the best thing to do is to return it to Mother Earth by burying it. It will take longer than your lifetime to heal these mistreated stones, but at least they can be returned to the womb of Mother Earth to be regenerated and transformed anew.

Although heat-treated citrine is the biggest offender among popular metaphysical stones, heat treatments are rampant in the world of fine gemstones. Known in the industry as *gemstone enhancement*, heat treatment alters the chemistry within stones like sapphire, topaz, and tourmaline, resulting in stones that are more saturated and intense in color. But these treatments wipe out the subtle hues and delicate wisps of color that once danced through the stones. The difference in their color before and after is like a meadow covered in delicate spring flowers versus its cartoon facsimile, drawn with heavy strokes and garish colors. But because many people consider subtle, understated hues to be drab, instead favoring saturated colors and their easy-to-see bold hues, they ignore the comparatively more understated tones gemstones naturally come in. Compounding this, large jewelry companies who sell the same designs in multiple stores take stones that naturally vary in hue and heat-treat them to become more uniform in color. This allows them to market and sell a consistent piece of jewelry throughout all their retail outlets. But as enticing as these jewels may be, the gemstones in them have been metaphysically impaired and are not useful to you as energetically healing jewelry.

DYED AND PAINTED STONES

There are regions where agates of muted and subtle color are found in vast quantity. These are considered "low-value" agates, for because of their comparatively plain appearance they do not garner the same attention as their more colorful agate counterparts. However, there is a way to make these understated agates more flashy: by dyeing them.

In order to make these agates colorful, they are put through a series of harsh chemical baths, some of which are quite poisonous. Their final color depends on the series of chemicals used, but all result in the absorption of gaudy bands of color where the dye is able to impregnate the stone. With the artificial treatment conveniently unmentioned, the eye-catching dyed-agate coasters, wind chimes, and bookends are then sold to unsuspecting, uninformed buyers, who, by omission of information, are led to believe they are natural stones.

Dyeing happens with other stones too. Turquoise can be an expensive semiprecious stone, but magnesite and howlite, both cream-colored stones, can be dyed to look like turquoise. Caveat emptor, for these are then sold to unsuspecting buyers who think they are getting a steal on real turquoise—but it is the buyers who are actually being fleeced.

Artificially dyed tumbled quartz

Other stones don't even get the effort of dyeing put into them and are coated in a layer of translucent paint. These stones will feel waxy to the touch, as though they have been very thinly coated with crayon. And as with dyed stones, the biggest tip-off is again a suspicious intensity and evenness in color.

IRRADIATED STONES

Unbelievably, things can get even worse when it comes to alterations made on crystals and stones.

Irradiating a crystal can change its color. But other than in the interest of scientific discovery, why would someone do this? Again, commerce plays a major role in the prevalence of this artificial treatment. For example, clear quartz is found in vast quantities all over the world. But with supply exceeding demand, new products are created in order to generate more profit, and one way this is done is by nuking quartz.

When clear quartz is exposed to millions of years of slow, natural radiation from Mother Earth, the aluminum impurities within its crystalline lattice are changed from clear to a tone of dark grayish brown to produce what is known as smoky quartz. But this effect can be artificially produced by placing quartz crystals in any machine that exposes them to radiation for a few hours, including nuclear reactors, particle accelerators, gamma ray machines, or even the X-ray machine at your local hospital. This results in quartz specimens with roots that may be white but with points in a saturated and overly homogenized hue of shiny blackish brown.

Unlike heat-treated citrine, which still has a modicum of manifestation energies, artificially irradiated smoky quartz sadly has zero metaphysical benefits. The accelerated process of irradiation distorts the natural energy of the quartz so that it no longer produces healing energies but causes

Artificially irradiated smoky quartz. Note how evenly saturated the dark tips are.

a forceful and hyperactive energy to come out of the crystal. Like a proverbial bull in a china shop (except in this case, a grotesque mutation of a bull on steroids), its energy lacks control and can't help but be destructive. It is no longer a healing stone.

But again, because of consumers' attraction to bright, gaudy colors, irradiation also happens regularly in the gemstone industry. Aquamarines, sapphires, rubies, diamonds, and topazes are among the stones that receive this damaging treatment because it causes the color of the stones to become more homogenized and saturated. This too is something to be avoided, for any unnatural irradiation nullifies the beneficial healing energy created by the gemstones. Instead, if you want to wear healing gems, seek out *natural gemstones*. Though they take a little more legwork to source, they can be found through independent jewelers whose stones are certified natural by gemstone laboratories. And unlike irradiated stones, natural gemstones will produce healing energies that benefit you.

ARTIFICIALLY COATED STONES

Any internet or social media hashtag search of "crystals" will result in millions of photos. And a significant portion of the top photos will show quartz-like crystals in a wide range of shimmering iridescent colors, with names like *Aqua Aura, Titanium Quartz, Angel Aura, Flame Aura, Gold Aura, Opal Aura,* and so on. That these photos rank so highly in the results is very sad, for it illustrates the popularity of crystals that have been permanently damaged by a process known as *vapor deposition*. This treatment is produced by placing crystals in a vacuum chamber heated to 1600°F. Then an aerosolized metal such as copper, gold, titanium, or niobium is added to the vacuum chamber. The atoms of metal fuse to the surface of the crystal, creating a permanent coating that cannot be removed.

This metal coating can be applied to many different minerals, but its most popular application is with quartz crystals. This is because quartz's shape with its varying faces shows the iridescence of the vapor deposition very well, but more importantly because cheap quartz is abundant and vapor deposition presents yet another way to make money from it. Unfortunately, crystals that have received this treatment are the metaphysical and mineralogical equivalent of cruelly treated factory-farmed

Iridescence with bold color is a key way to identify crystals that have been energetically damaged by a process called vapor deposition. The other way is if a crystal has "aura" in its name. For example, Angel Aura, Aqua Aura, Gold Aura, Rose Aura, and Sunset Aura are all crystals that have undergone this artificial process.

chickens. Honor is not given to the animals in the factory farm, and honor is not given to stones subjected to this process. So violent is vapor deposition that the heating process alone can cause quartzes to explode, destroying themselves and neighboring crystals in the process.

Additionally, vapor deposition is not in any way, shape, or form a spiritual process. The main clients of vapor deposition are in industries like aerospace, automotive, and optics. It is the same process used to coat semiconductors for electronics, make firearms more durable, and manufacture the silvery lining in potato chip bags. Clearly, none of these products have any connection to spirituality or healing. But because of either devious marketing or unquestioning acceptance by the metaphysical community, these crystals have taken over the crystal healing market. These purported metaphysical crystals with their colorful iridescent coatings come with the claim that the vapor deposition process is an "alchemical fusion" of technology and nature.

I call bullshit.

These crystals are not created by true alchemy, nor are they metaphysical crystals.

In fact, the metaphysical properties of the stones have been permanently destroyed.

If I attempt to tune in to stones that have had this treatment, I am unable to pick up anything because information comes through muffled and distorted, as though it has been filtered through bad audio processing. What the stones originally wanted to communicate I am now unable to hear, for their voices have now been blocked by a coating of metal. The special doorways of information found through natural etchings on a crystal's surface are now forever covered. The healing energy that would have been projected by their turbo-boosting spirals has now been halted. The only way to remove the coating is to grind it off, which would also grind into the crystal, damaging it. With vapor deposition, the crystal loses its power to heal, and you lose the ability to receive its healing.

Ironically, the reason these crystals are so popular is precisely because of people's interest in crystal healing. Within the psyche, there is a subconscious recognition of the power of the quartz shape. But it's the scintillating iridescent colors that people consciously gravitate to. If you have not yet developed your intuitive abilities and are not yet able to discern energy coming from the crystals, you will default to purely visual cues, like color and iridescence, to alert you to a stone's power. But just as with fancy packaging, it's only the superficial appearance that you are responding to.

This is why bold, unnaturally colored crystals are so popular. It is a reflection of the common but incorrect belief that metaphysical energies are distinct and loud, like bold colors. But this is not what metaphysical energies feel like. On a scale from one to ten, where the tangibility of physical experiences would rate as a ten, metaphysical energies, far more faint, would rate at one. But because many people don't know this, they think that psychic energies will have the same sort of intense tactility they experience in the physical life. Thus they look for some sort of distinct physical cue to tell them a stone is powerful, and most often this is through bold, ostentatious color.

The recommendation of artificially coated stones can be a litmus test to determine whether or not a "crystal expert" is truly in the service of the crystals. If they advocate the use of and purport the metaphysical properties of crystals like these, I immediately know they are not in true, deep connection with crystalline energy.

Vapor deposition can be applied to a wide range of
minerals—even non-mineral objects. Here, several kinds
of quartz, obsidian, kyanite, danburite—even a poor dried
seahorse—have had an artificial coating of aerosolized
titanium applied to them.

This is called goldstone and I'm baffled by people who purport it to have healing powers. It's just manufactured glass with glitter in it.

This means that in order to harness her energies you must utilize the tools she has created and not "minerals" unconsciously made by man.

I know this chapter has been depressing, but it's important to learn how your desire to use crystalline energies has been deliberately used against you. Though this information has been harsh, by learning how the crystals have been tampered with you can become aware of other kinds of minefields you must learn to navigate when pursuing metaphysical knowledge. For unfortunately, the spiritual and metaphysical worlds are rife with charlatans—some unwitting, others deliberately so; and whether this happens on purpose, due to inexperience, or because of someone's self-inflated ego, you can be misled. But do not despair, for your desire to have a deeper, more personal connection with crystals has led you to this book, and through your journey with them you will find the path that helps you to discern the spiritual integrity of others while discovering your own spiritual truth.

Though you may already be eager to go out and get crystals to work with, choosing the right crystals is not only knowing about what crystals *not* to get. Instead of rushing out and buying some crystals right now, what you actually need is to first learn how crystals work with *your* energies. In the subsequent chapters, you will learn how to work with crystals in a deeper and more conscientious way, and this will greatly illuminate your awareness of their energies. Instead of needlessly spending energy and money on crystals you won't really use or need, by the end of the book you will have the ability to determine which crystals will be the best and most powerful crystals for you.

These are lab-created stones. Quartz, ametrine, sapphire, emerald, and tourmaline can all be made artificially in a lab; labs even manufacture minerals that are never found in nature (such as the orange stone shown here). Clockwise from left to right: lab-created quartz, ametrine, phokenite, chalcanthite, tourmaline, emerald, and sapphire.

OPPOSITE: Red Jasper conglomerate   ABOVE: Chipboard Rhyolite
(aka Jelly Bean Jasper)

Rainbow obsidian cabochon

This fluorite has been cut into a six-sided point,
but this was done to feature the intricate and
beautiful bands of color within the crystal.
This kind of thoughtfulness and craftsmanship
gives honor and respect to the stone.

Quartz carved into platonic solids

These quartz ventifacts have been
naturally carved and polished by wind.

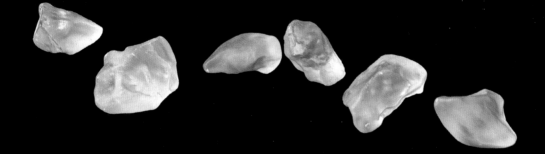

CHAPTER 7

DEVELOPING YOUR OWN RELATIONSHIP WITH THE CRYSTALS

THERE ARE ESSENTIALLY TWO WAYS of understanding the metaphysical properties of crystals. The first is to read what others have written. Numerous crystal books and online resources exist that list crystals and their metaphysical properties. With a little research, you can find thousands of crystal descriptions for many different stones, from the very common to the ultrarare.

Although this is a quick and easy way to access information, it comes with some serious caveats. The biggest issue is that *it's someone else's information*. Relying on this method means that you are fully dependent on someone else's interpretation of crystalline energy. But not all people who channel crystals have the ability, integrity, and/or humility to accurately communicate a stone's metaphysical properties, and instead they may disseminate inaccurate or faulty information about the stones. Another issue is with stone availability. While some mines have such large quantities of a particular mineral that it remains in constant supply, other stones can be found only in one small geological pocket, so the specimens are limited in quantity. Since the supply of crystals is unpredictable and constantly shifting, many crystal encyclopedias end up referencing stones that have, over time, become very difficult to find. The downside to this is that a crystal seeker may read about a stone and become fixated on it, believing that the specific crystal is the only way to access a certain type of metaphysical support. But the stone they seek may now be so rare and in demand that they are unable to find it, or if they do, its price may be out of reach. Without the stone, the crystal seeker fears they will never be able to get the support they need.

So what do you do?

Try the second (and best) way of understanding the metaphysical properties of crystals: *Develop your own intuition with the crystals*.

By developing your own intuition you'll discover that you already have a deep and profound connection with the stones. Instead of relying on someone else's description of a crystal, you are able to channel information about the stone yourself. You will find you are neither dependent on someone else's experience of a stone, nor are you limited to the stones that have previously been written about. You can then discover the metaphysical properties of any stone you encounter, including the thousands that have had little to nothing written about them. Thus you will also be able to bypass the problem of needing a specific stone, for you will be easily able to find other stones that can help you equally, or even better.

But like taking the training wheels off your bike, this method requires a big leap of faith—and lots of practice. You may be wobbly at first, unsure of the information you're channeling, but with practice you will be able to rely on your own intuitive strength and balance to support yourself. And this book has been written to help you gain the strength to do just that.

THE BLIND MEN AND THE ELEPHANT

Before you begin the journey of developing your crystal intuition, let me share with you a parable:

> *A group of blind men surround an elephant. As they touch it, they tell each other what they feel an elephant is. One man describes the elephant's trunk, while another tells of its thick legs. A third speaks about the elephant's ears, while yet another talks about its tail. None of their descriptions are quite the same.*

Although in the parable each blind man describes the elephant a bit differently, none of them is wrong in their description. They each have described their true experience of the elephant. It's the same when one intuitively connects with the crystals.

You may not pick up the same information that someone else picks up about a stone, but this does not mean that your personal experience is wrong. Like the blind men in the parable, who are each positioned at a specific part of the elephant, the unique harmonics of your energy cause you to be "placed" at a different perspective than anyone else. The information you get from the stone may not describe the "whole elephant," but you are able to describe the energetic part of the crystal you're closest to.

While my job as a crystal healer is to understand and to help communicate to others the larger picture of a stone's properties (the "whole elephant"), you need to know only how the stones work for you. The perspective you have on the crystal, and the intuitive information you get from it, is not an accident, for you are in the exact position to pick up the information you need about the stone. As time goes on and as the harmonics of your energy deepen and evolve, more information will be revealed to you—especially as you continue working with the same stone! And though you will draw your own conclusions about each crystal, as you compare notes with others you'll be interested to find that you're picking up on the same themes—though sometimes on different tangents. Your friend may experience the "trunk" while you get the "tail"; but though each of you is experiencing the energy from a different perspective, the information will connect together. You both may have to work with the stone for a bit before you pick up enough details to see the overlap, but the overlap is there.

POTATO VERSUS POTATO

In addition to being positioned in a way that allows you to receive the information you most need, the energy of the crystal collaborates with your unique energy. Let's return to a cooking analogy to help you understand this concept:

Q: If we both had a potato, would we cook the same potato dish?
A: Not necessarily.

Maybe you're in the mood for mashed potatoes, and I want some french fries. Or maybe you want a potato salad and I want some crispy potato tacos. Though it's the same ingredient, it can be used in a multitude of ways. *Ditto with crystals!*

Each and every crystal has different potential depending on the interaction of the crystal's energies with your own energy and predilections. As in the cooking analogy, you may start with something easy, like making a lot of mashed potatoes. But as you become more comfortable and confident, you'll begin trying other recipes that intrigue you. With experience and experimentation, you'll discover exactly what kind of potato dishes you enjoy most. This is the same process you'll go through to develop your personal understanding of each crystal.

SURPRISE YOURSELF WITH WHAT YOU ALREADY KNOW

The development of your crystal intuition will be a lifelong process (well, actually, technically, it's already been a multilife process), so you shouldn't worry about immediately understanding the complete properties of a stone. Your most important and primary job is to learn how each crystal works for you so you can understand how it can help and heal you. So take a leap of faith with your intuitive abilities. As long as you try your best, you'll surprise yourself with how much you already know.

Manganoan calcite is an example of a mineral that will exhibit
a different color under UV light. Above, it is shown under
natural light; at right, fluorescing under shortwave UV light.

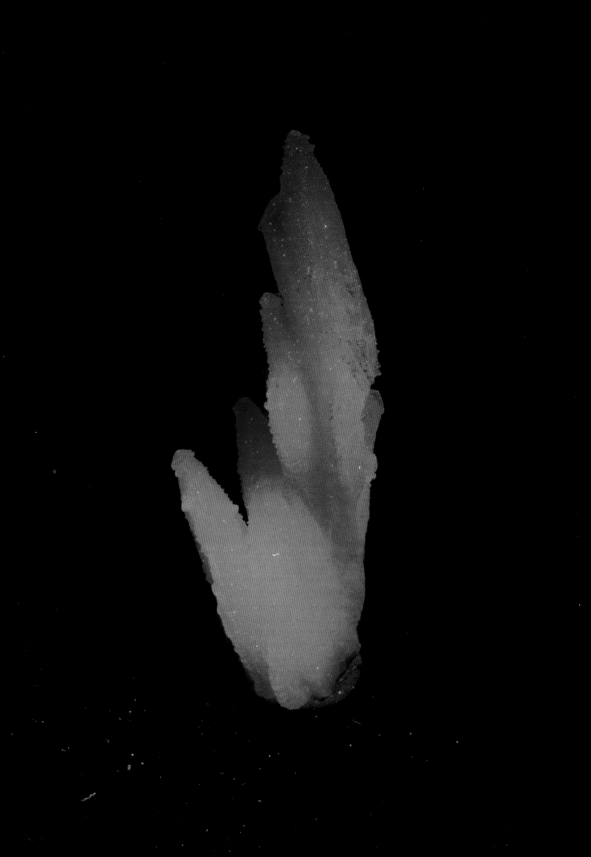

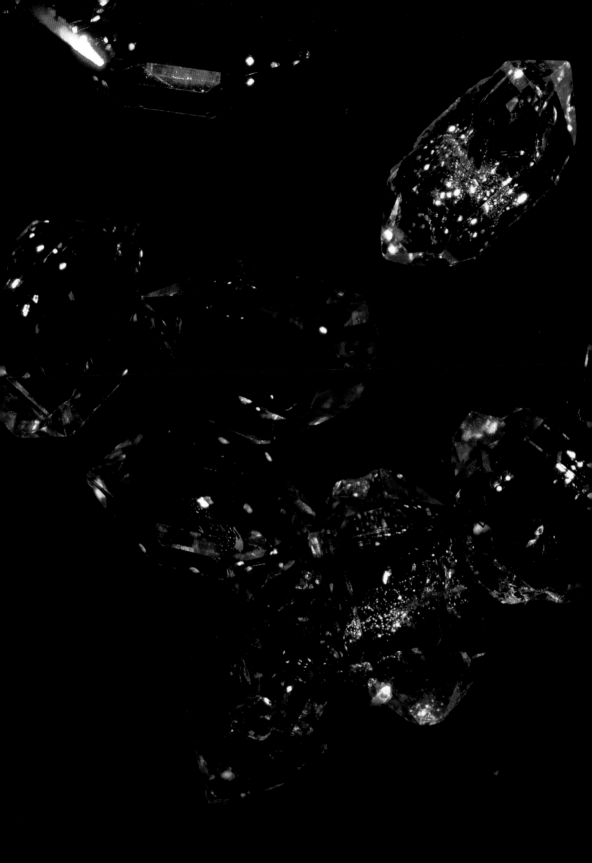

Double-pointed quartz crystals with petroleum inclusions. Petroleum fluoresces under UV light, highlighting the bubbles of methane trapped within the liquid.

CHAPTER 8

HOW TO TAP INTO
YOUR INTUITION

MOVIES SHOW PSYCHIC ABILITY in grandiose ways. Suddenly, a psychic is struck by a vision. Frozen in a trance, with the back of one hand on their forehead, they begin seeing visions of people and objects in graphic detail. A ghost speaks to a psychic, and the psychic hears the ghost's words in coherent linear sentences. Or a psychic knocks books off of shelves, slides cars across the street, and throws people off cliffs solely with her powers of telekinesis!

Like so much of real life, intuition is nothing like what's shown in movies. But because TV and films are the way most people are exposed to "psychic" ability, their understanding of it can be distorted. While these portrayals make for entertaining, dramatic scenes, they create misconceptions of how one actually receives intuitive impressions and how psychic ability truly works. Although the depictions have a small grain of truth, compared to reality, they are massive exaggerations. Like the famous filmmaking adage "Movies are life with the boring parts cut out," true intuitive ability contains lots of "boring" parts. So if you have been looking for your intuition to present itself in a big, intense way, you've been missing it, for the majority of intuitive impressions are quiet and seemingly mundane. Thus, getting in touch with your intuition means letting go of expectations that your psychic ability will be anything like what you've seen on the big screen. Instead, it requires you to shift your focus into a subtle frequency where information often comes in glimpses and segments. And because you are unique, the way the intuitive information presents itself to you will be unique as well.

Though the word *clairvoyant* has been used as a catchall for psychic ability, the combination of its root words actually means "clear sight." But clairvoyance specifically applies to the ability to "see" psychic impressions; that is, to get intuitive impressions visually through images and pictures. There is also *clairaudience*, meaning "clear hearing," which is the ability to receive intuitive impressions through your psychic ears. *Clairsentience* refers to receiving intuitive information via your physical body through feelings, emotions, and other bodily sensations. Being *empathic* is a more specific form of clairsentience; you are intuiting the feelings, emotions, and bodily sensations that another person or being is experiencing. *Claircognizance* applies to those who just "know" information without any influence of outside information, facts, or logic. You can even be *clairgustant*, which means you get psychic information from smelling or tasting things, or *clairalient*, which means you can smell or taste things psychically!

Just as some people are naturally talented singers while others are gifted mechanics, athletes, or doctors, you too have natural intuitive talents. Though one of these sixth senses will be your strongest, it won't be your only one. You will always have other "clairs" supporting you. And it is this unique combination of senses that gives you a fuller range of intuitive perception.

YOU ARE INTUITIVE

I cannot emphasize this enough: *Everyone has intuitive ability*. But the key to developing your abilities is understanding how your intuition works. Whereas some people have been born fully aware of their intuitive talents, others are karmically born into families, societies, or situations that actively suppress their intuitive abilities. Others are born into circumstances where intuitive abilities are not believed to exist. So until these people are able to access the information and training to develop their talents, their abilities will lie hidden, waiting to be discovered.

At this moment you may already know which sixth sense you favor. However, to make this ability more distinct and the information you receive from it clearer, you have to strengthen it. And then by developing your strongest intuitive ability, you will strengthen your other intuitive senses as well. The more you practice, the more skilled you will become, and you will gain abilities that you can never lose. Like wisdom, they will stay with you forever.

UNDERSTANDING HOW YOUR INTUITION SPEAKS TO YOU

Core to developing your intuition is understanding symbology.

A symbol can be interpreted through its *universal meaning*. For instance, the symbol of a heart universally represents love. The symbol of a house universally represents home or life at home. The color white often represents perfection, cleanliness, and the angelic realm. These examples are symbols with generally agreed-upon meanings, the kind of descriptions listed in dream dictionaries.

However, these are only generalized meanings of the symbols. Your personal relationship with each and every symbol is far deeper and more nuanced than any explanation that can be found in a book. For example, most people would agree that the butterfly is a symbol of transformation, but I have a cousin who loathes butterflies because of how erratically they fly. When she sees a butterfly, she sees something that is out of control. Thus, the symbol of a butterfly has a different *personal meaning* to her than it would for most.

Another example: The cross is known as the symbol of the Christian religion. But depending on your take on Christianity, the cross can represent the overwhelming love and grace of Christ consciousness or the energy of judgment, intolerance, and extreme dogma. If you were a medieval Mongol, the Christian cross would represent the sacred directions of north, south, east, and west.

Thus the personal meanings of your symbols are influenced by your own experience and the culture you grew up in. For instance, if you were born into a Western culture, a white house could symbolize cleanliness and perfection within a home, while if you grew up in an Asian culture, the color white might mean mourning and death, making your interpretation of the symbol of a white house "home of death." If you happen to be someone with both cultures influencing your life, a closer look at the details of the symbol can offer clues to help you determine if the white color is in reference to Asian or Western culture or, perhaps, to your own personal symbolism. For example, the white house may be Chinese in style, or perhaps mid-century California modern, or the color of a dollhouse you once had. In each case, your personal relationship to the symbol would greatly influence its meaning. And noticing how the different details interact provides additional information to glean from the symbol as well.

Unraveling your personal meanings helps sort through the information hidden within your symbols so that you are able to see how your intuition likes to communicate with you. And by knowing your personal symbols you are able to access your talents in other divinatory arts. For example: One way crystal balls are used for divinatory readings is through symbology. Much like finding shapes in passing clouds, some crystal ball readers look for symbols in the layers of wisps, bubbles, and inclusions within the interior of the crystal ball. Once they see a symbol, they reference their own personal symbol dictionary to decipher its meaning and convey this information to the recipient. This technique of seeing symbols within a physical medium is known as scrying and is also the basis of divinatory readings that use tea leaves, coffee grounds, a fire's flames, smoke, water, and even patterns of light dancing on walls. In every method, the reader looks for symbols. But the only symbols that will appear will be the ones that the reader has a personal connection to—otherwise the symbol will not appear to them at all.

Understanding your personal symbols is also essential to interpreting your dreams. When you are physically awake, your perception is focused on linear time. But in the dream state, time is flexible. You can move forward and backward in time with relative ease—the hallmark of multidimensional experience. But the seemingly random experiences happening in your dream state are actually multidimensional information that has been compressed to fit your linear perception. Since it is your dream, it uses your symbols, which makes you the best person to unpack it and make sense of what it was trying to tell you.

So now that you understand how important your personal symbols are, it is time to begin recording the symbols that appear in your life.

You've actually already done this. . . .

Learning to Tap into Your Intuition

WARNING: If you have not done the previous exercises, stop here. Go back and do all the exercises in order!

Now that you have done the previous exercises, it's time to take them to the next level! Remember your observation notes for exercise 1 (page 24) ? Although it was an exercise in observation, it was also secretly an exercise in picking up symbols! Here's what to do now:

1. Go back to your list and begin circling all the "symbols" you saw. Circle every object, color, sound, tactile experience—basically, anything that could be interpreted as a symbol. If you have adjectives that further describe something, as in the phrase "blue house," circle that as a whole symbol.

2. On another page, create two columns. In the left-hand column, write down the list of symbols that you saw. For compound symbols (like "blue house") write down "blue house," "blue," and "house" each as separate symbols.

3. In the right-hand column, write down what each corresponding symbol personally means to you. Notes to help you:

- If you've written down "red," try and remember what kind of red you saw. If you don't remember, that's okay. But if you do, note what shade it was. Then, in column 2, do your best to clarify what the specific color means to you.

- Colors also affect the meanings of objects they are paired with. (While alone "cherry red" may mean "adolescent fun," and "car" may represent "a way to travel from one place to another," the combination of the two symbols into "cherry-red car" may produce an entirely different meaning, like "car for someone who likes to show off.")

- Similarly, if you've written down "slate-blue house" as a symbol, elaborate further on its specific details. A "Victorian slate-blue house" will have a different meaning than a "modernist slate-blue house."

- Add to column 2 how each individual object/symbol makes you feel. If an object makes you feel happy, ask yourself what kind of happiness you feel. "Kid on Christmas morning" happy, or "I get to sleep in on Saturday" happy—these are different kinds of happiness. You'll get more information out of your symbol if you distinguish the exact shade of feeling you get from it.

4. Do a second pass. See if you can "squeeze out" deeper information about your symbols. Write down everything, even if it doesn't make sense now. Notes to help you:

- One way to get into the deeper meaning of the symbol is to **become** the symbol. Close your eyes and inhabit the symbol. If you wrote down "pigeon," imagine turning into the pigeon you saw. When you take its form, do you get a better sense of what it/you represent?

- Each symbol always has additional layers of information. The more you explore them, the more information you will be able to extract. One way you can do this is by free-associating your symbols with memories from your life. For instance: If you wrote down "cherry-red car," recall any situation that it reminds you of. Perhaps it makes you think of a car that you once admired, or of a boy you knew in school who had one, or maybe even a toy car you used to play with. Then ask yourself what you associate with the circumstance. Maybe the cherry-red car you admired was one you had wanted to own, the boy with the cherry-red car was someone you had a crush on, or you got to play with a cherry-red toy car when you visited your cousins out of state. Connected to your symbols are memories that are loaded with information to glean. So if you find yourself thinking of the boy with the cherry-red car, you could think about how you felt about the boy, what about him you gravitated toward, how you felt about yourself at that time of your life, and what your takeaway is now that you can look back at your life. By connecting your symbols to past experiences, you are able to go deeper into your symbols and glean richer information from them.

Continuing the same example used in exercise 2 (page 48), the following is an abbreviated excerpt of a few of the symbols deciphered by this person:

SYMBOL	PERSONAL MEANING
STREET	Traveling, getting from a to b, a journey
Two-way street	More possibilities, more directions to take
Two-way traffic	Movement in both directions, you can go either way
TRAFFIC LIGHT	A bit more urgent and "in your face" than a stop sign
Alternating light	Pay attention, be aware
Red and green light	"There are times to move forward and times to be where you are."
Red light	Warning, stop, not a good idea
Green light	Cheerful, signaling it is safe to move forward in chosen direction
TREES	Life, growth, they reach upward, endure all kinds of weather, grow, adapt, they have roots to feed and stabilize themselves
Trees lining the sidewalk	Comforting feeling, life is there and is growing, it's not a wasteland
Trees on both sides of the street	Double the fun, the more the merrier, more oxygenated air for us, "we work together"
Green foliage	Green is life!
Mixed colors of green foliage	Younger leaves are brighter, peridot colored, "newbies"; literally "green"/inexperienced; older leaves are deeper in color, a kelly green, a color that is more experienced and knowledgeable; the mixture of colors represents a community of new and old
Full foliage	Community, living together and receiving nutrients from the same source, harmony
Old trees	Wisdom, endurance, loving beings, they have seen a lot
Trees cracking the sidewalks with their roots	Causing twists in the road, but you are still able to walk on top of them

SYMBOL	PERSONAL MEANING
SIDEWALKS	Passageways, paths, always leading to a possibility, going somewhere
Cracks in sidewalks	Changes, as things in the path that are encountered, a bump in the road
Roots (in sidewalks)	Sustainability, stability
PARKING METERS WITH PARKED CARS	A busy street where people are stopping, stops along the road
Parking meter	Measurement of allotted time
Parked cars	Choosing to stay for a bit
Small, compact cars	Saves on gas and money, easier for city parking
APARTMENT	Not staying as long, not committed to a mortgage, the ability to leave easily if they want
Apartment with red-and-black sign	A possibility for grounding, but be aware of any red flags
Red	Stop, warning, take notice, strength
Black	Solid, grounding
BREEZE	Gentle, comforting, feels good on the skin
Soft breeze	Movement, sometimes relief from a hot day
PEOPLE WALKING BY	People moving through their lives, available to meet others, lives crossing for brief moments
People of different ages, races, genders, clothing	Beauty of all kinds of people living together
People speaking in multiple languages	It's like "music" with different inflections and rhythms

SYMBOL	PERSONAL MEANING
DOG ON LEASH WITH OWNER IN A RED DRESS	Owner with strong, confident, commanding personality, dog does not really have to be on a leash, but owner is being respectful of others
Red dress	Cherry-red is a take-notice, confident color, like the "Here I am!" dress of Scarlett O'Hara
Leash	Provides safety as a seatbelt to a car, prefer the connection with my dog off-leash as it is one of mutual understanding, respect, and trust
Terrier	Small, wiry, can hold its own despite size
Middle-aged dog	Laid back, not puppy energy but not so old it cannot get out and do stuff
SMALL PURSE DOG ON LEASH WITH OLDER WOMAN	A person who has more life experience, is not on their own, has a connection to another being
Small purse dog	Purse dogs are portable companions, happy bouncy friends
Dog on leash	Keeping companion safe. Teaching, training, best practices
Older woman with good posture, wearing blue denim capris and tennis shoes	Not in corporate world. Retired or on the brink of it. Enjoying her life now. Woman who has a sense of self, peace, and freedom. I see a little bit of myself in her.
Older woman	A person who has been around
Good body posture	Feeling positive, not depressed. A healthy, vital look
Denim	Durable, all-purpose
Tennis shoes	Shoes worn for movement

Now that you have thoroughly completed the exercises, it's time to reveal the magic to yourself. Remember exercise 3 (page 134), when you wrote down a question about your life? Pull it out and look at it alongside the list of symbols and meanings you just made.

Do you see a relationship between your question and the symbols you just deciphered?

Do you see how you answered your own question?

Can you now see how intuitive you already are?

CHAPTER 9

UNDERSTANDING YOUR INTUITION AND HOW IT WORKS WITH CRYSTALS

BEFORE WE CONTINUE ON to developing your intuition, I want to highlight a significant point about the last exercise: Even if a dozen people looked at the exact same scene, *no one would make the same list of symbols*. Each person will notice different things, because what catches a person's attention depends on how the world looks through their eyes. This is because how you observe the world is just as unique as you are and the symbols you will notice are the ones that contain the information you most need. As with the blind men and the elephant (page 199), your intuitive perspective has put you in a position to see the symbols that are most relevant to you.

If you had trouble seeing the connection between your symbols and your question, don't worry. Sometimes developing your intuitive abilities is like searching all over for your keys, when all along they've been in your hands. Your expectations of what intuition is supposed to look and feel like can keep you from seeing the information that is right in front of you. Though the intuitive information is there, your determination to see it in a particular way prevents it from coming into focus for you. But as long as the question you posed was clear, there are several ways you can help yourself unravel the information that is within your symbols.

Sometimes all one needs to do is to go deeper into a symbol's meaning. For example, once, while doing the previous exercise in a workshop, one participant could not make sense of how her symbols related to her question. She mentioned that she had seen a clear blue sky and birds flying in the air, and knew that these symbols were related to the feeling of lightness and spaciousness. But she was still unable to see how it related to her question, "What is going on in my romantic relationship?"

As soon as I asked her to sink deep into the feeling of the birds flying in the sky, she began to cry. She realized that the lightness and spaciousness she felt when embodying these birds felt like freedom, something she wasn't fully aware she was craving. Her relationship had been in turmoil. Though she cared for her partner and was doing what she could to keep the relationship together, in that moment it dawned on her how much she longed for freedom.

Simply by delving into the feeling of her symbol, she was able to *experience* its meaning rather than have only a conceptual understanding of what her symbol meant. Unraveling her symbols also helped her reveal her innermost truth to herself. Not only did the exercise answer her original question, it also gave her information on how she needed to proceed with her relationship. And all this information was compressed within two symbols.

Another thing you can do to make the information in your symbols clearer is to expand your awareness. We all have particular things we tend to focus on when we look around us. For example, when I have done the observation exercise (exercise 2, page 48) in workshops, I have discovered that while some students will tend only to notice buildings, others only see plants and other objects in nature, and some seem to be aware only of people and the activities they are doing. This tendency to focus only on certain categories is common, but it illustrates how narrow one's field of vision can be. This happens because it's a way for you to subconsciously filter out aspects of life that you don't want to look at or see. It's one thing to be drawn to a particular subject/area and notice it first, but if you don't "see" anything else, it means that your perception has been limited. But if you can practice expanding your awareness to other categories of objects you aren't normally inclined to pay attention to, your perception will broaden and you will be aware of more symbols that can be interpreted. This will result in a much wider range of symbols to glean information from.

Another reason why the previous exercise may have been challenging has to do with your prior experience with intuition. If you are someone who is already connected to their intuition, you may have expected this exercise to feel like what you usually experience. But the practice of decoding symbols can be very different from the intuitive experiences of "gut feelings" and psychic "impressions." In fact, the example used in exercises 2 and 4 (pages 48 and 214) was written by an energy

driving dreams would be frustrating: I would be stuck in traffic or literally driving up a vertical wall to get where I needed to go. But as the dreams kept reoccurring, it began to dawn on me that these dreams were showing me important symbolic information about how I was moving through my life.

I eventually determined that to me "driving" symbolized movement from one place to another. I recognized that it was faster than walking but covered less ground than being on a plane. But at least with driving I was still the one navigating and in control. My white Civic was my first new car, and as a teenager living at home, jonesing for freedom and with a deep desire to go forth into the world, the car became a representation both of myself and of all the hopes and dreams I had for my life at that time.

The other details in these dreams would reveal to me information about the circumstances I was in and how I was handling them. When my dreams were about driving like a skilled race car driver, they were showing me that I was also skillfully navigating the situations around me in my waking life. When my dreams were about being behind some slow-moving vehicle, they were showing me that I happened to be dealing with a slow-moving person or situation. When I found myself in awe and amazement as I dreamed of defying gravity and driving up a wall, my dream was telling me that I was doing something I had thought was impossible—while also telling me I was feeling as if I was going crazy for doing it. Each detail gave me clues that helped me navigate my life and showed me when I was (too often) pushing against a situation.

Many years later, long after I had stopped having dreams about driving my white Civic, I stumbled across a page in an old dream journal. In it, I wrote of a deeply frustrating dream where I was driving to some destination in Los Angeles, only to get stuck in total gridlock. Though the next freeway exit was only a few cars ahead, as far as I could see, every car in every lane was packed bumper to bumper with no room to move. I was so close to the exit, but because I was completely surrounded on all sides by cars there was no way I could get off the freeway. All I could do was wait in frustration until traffic began to move again. And because traffic was the worst I had ever seen, it was going to be a very long wait.

At the time of this dream, one of my greatest aspirations was to move to Los Angeles. I felt a distinct connection between this desire and the dream I had had, and in both my physical and dream life I felt the intense disappointment of my goals being delayed. I hadn't wanted to hear it, but I knew my dream was telling me that my life goals were not moving on my schedule and that my only choice was to wait things out. And indeed, my dream of moving to Los Angeles was delayed many more years, and I spent the interim futilely fighting the circumstances of my life instead of making the most of the situation I was in.

I had already been happily settled in Los Angeles for some years when I rediscovered the journal entry. As I reread it, I found myself gobsmacked by all the information that had been hidden in plain sight and finally understood what all the symbols in my dream had been about. For in my dream, the freeway exit that was only a few cars ahead of me, the exit that I would have gotten off at out of angst and restlessness had I had the chance, the exit that I knew in the dream was not my intended destination, *was the same freeway exit before the actual exit to my first Los Angeles apartment.*

When I had my dream, I had no idea that it contained information about my future, only that it was confirming what was happening in my life at the time. Even though I had forgotten about it, the dream had been so intense that when I was reminded of it, I could both instantly and viscerally recall how it made me feel. The potency of my feelings within the dream had been even more intense than the memories I had about that time of my life, when I had felt like I was constantly moving, yet going nowhere. And all this intuitive information, with relevance for me both back then and in the future, had been compressed within the symbols of one dream. It just took quite a bit of time before I could finally understand what my dream was telling me: that I had been *very close to my goal* (the exit to my first apartment) but that it was *going to take time* (traffic) to get to my destination because I was in *circumstances greater than me* (massive gridlock).

Now I rarely dream of driving, and when I do I'm not driving like a frantic teenager. The intervening years of experience have given me more wisdom to understand that movement doesn't necessarily equate with progress, and I now better understand how to go with the flow of life while still being in control in the driver's seat. When I do happen to dream of driving, I take note, because these dreams always have a significant relationship to those I had as a teen. Every so often a driving dream will return to show me how I am currently moving through life, with each model of car I drive giving me different information. If I happen to be driving a white car (as I had as a teen), I pay attention to any angst I might be feeling, for my dream is reminding me to be aware of any old, unproductive habits that may be returning. If I do dream of my old Honda, it can be an even louder warning to take notice of my life. Or if I happen to be driving a current model car like a responsible adult, it is showing me just how far along I have come with my patience.

24/7 ACCESS

As you can see, symbols hold the key to accessing the intuitive information that is around you. And now you have symbols from your last exercise that you can add to your personal symbol dictionary. In addition to helping you connect to your intuition, your symbol dictionary can be used for scrying or interpreting your dreams. The more effort you put into deciphering your symbols, the more you will notice them around you and the more intuitive information you will be able to interpret from them. As time goes on and as you continue adding details to your personal symbol dictionary, you will discover deeper meanings within them, and each variation of your symbol will shed light on the general meaning of your symbol on the whole. As your symbols come up again and again, you will begin to see significant relationships developing between them. These relationships will also impart additional intuitive information.

All of this is why you want to take the time to go deep into your symbols. For any direction you go further into gives you additional information to work with. And this will only serve to make your intuitive insights clearer to you. It will also show you the massive amount of intuitive information that can be found at any time and in any place, even in the tiniest of details. And your continual exploration of your symbols will help you better trust your own intuitive abilities. Though it takes more effort, your personal symbol dictionary will always be vastly more useful than some generic dictionary of symbols.

UNDERSTANDING YOUR INTUITIVE STRENGTHS

Look at your list of observations from exercise 2 (page 48) again. In addition to your visual observations, did you find that you wrote a lot about sounds you heard, like the music coming out of someone's car or the sound of the leaves in the wind? Or did you observe how warm and humid the air felt or that the bus bench across the street looked hard to sit on? Or did you perhaps smell cinnamon pastries baking in the shop next door?

If you noticed that you favored one sense over another in your descriptions of the world you observed, this can give insight into which of your clairs, or intuitive abilities, you are likely to be most dominant with. Again, it's important to know that you have abilities with all your different clairs but that some may be stronger than others. Being aware of what kind of symbols you tend to pick up will help give you an indication of which of your intuitive clairs you most gravitate to.

Distinguishing, and then developing, your intuitive strengths helps you understand what your psychic forte happens to be. For not only do you have a strength with a certain sixth sense, you also have particular psychic gifts. You may discover you have a natural affinity for psychically communicating with animals or the ability to psychically diagnose medical issues. Perhaps you discover you have a special affinity for communicating with spirits who have crossed over or an ability to communicate with angels. Maybe your strength is reading and interpreting tarot cards or finding lost objects. There are hundreds of psychic specialties that you could discover you have a talent for.

You can always acquire skills in any psychic specialty you have interest in, even if it's not your natural strength. In the same way that one can get better at playing guitar, speed reading, whittling wood carvings, or playing Ultimate Frisbee, one can better one's skills in any psychic niche, including understanding, communicating, and working with crystals!

PSYCHOMETRY

Psychometry is the intuitive reading of the energy and information about an object through physical touch. It is a psychic specialty most often associated with gathering information about an object's past history or the person who owned the object. But psychometry can also be used to sense the metaphysical energies an object produces—like the energies of crystals!

The psychometric information you pick up from the crystals will be more abstract than what you would receive by intuiting historical information about an object. Historical information will be more literal, while crystalline information will be more ethereal and symbolic. **So it's important not to prejudge your responses.** More often than not, the intuitive impressions you blow off as being insignificant or something you think you've made up will be the most accurate and insightful. The exercise that follows is one I teach in my workshop, and I can't tell you how many times someone didn't write down an impression because they assumed it wasn't compelling enough— only to find out their intuition was right on target! **So write everything down!**

Also, utilize all your different clairs. Follow every thought, feeling, and sound you hear in your head and see where it takes you. Write down each seemingly random thought and memory that pops into your mind. Write down how you feel emotionally, even if the feeling is fleeting. Write down what you feel in your body and where you feel it. If you feel a gesture moving through your body, explain what it feels most like. Sometimes all you will get is a word. Write it all down!

This next exercise is about developing your intuition and making it sharper. Worrying about getting information "right" defeats the purpose, as intuition does not work in that way. Instead, developing your intuition means becoming more accurate, detailed, and clear about the impressions you are receiving. If you happen to find this exercise difficult, it means that you are trying too hard to get the "right" answers instead of allowing your impressions to move through you. Don't worry about being wrong or about whether or not you have psychometric abilities. Remember, this is a practice to **develop** your abilities, so be gentle on yourself. Relaxing will actually make you more receptive to your intuition.

Ready to discover how *you* connect with the crystals?

Training with the Stones

WARNING: If you have not acquired the stones (see page 21) and done the previous exercises, go back and do them all in order. You'll be forever changed by what you learn here, so make the most of the surprise for yourself. It will be worth it!

You will need:

- The three unknown stones, separately wrapped and marked A, B, and C
- The sealed envelope identifying your secret crystals
- A timer
- A notebook

PART ONE

1. Place the package marked "A" in your hand. It doesn't matter which hand you hold the stone with. But do not squeeze the package to estimate the shape or texture of the stone.

2. Set a timer for five minutes, and begin writing down your intuitive impressions. Write down in a single column anything and everything that comes to you. A few tips:

- You don't necessarily want to write down the purely physical impressions you have of the stone (e.g., how heavy or light it feels). Instead, you want to write down your *intuitive* impressions of the stone. Again, these impressions will come through as a seemingly random stream of thoughts, feelings, and memories. Go with it and remember not to censor yourself.

- If after a few minutes you find yourself tapped out of thoughts, switch the stone to your other hand. This may trigger more information to come through to you.

- If you still seem out of thoughts, just sit quietly with the stone. You want to reach a point where you are no longer overfocusing on the stone. Relaxing allows for more information to come through.

3. Create your glossary. Next to the impressions you wrote, write down what they mean to you. Go through the impressions just like you did with the symbols in exercise 4 (page 214).

4. Repeat steps 1 through 3 with the additional packages.

5. Open only the sealed envelopes identifying the stones. **Leave the stones sealed for now. Turn to the Crystal Index** (page 328) for a summary of each stone's properties. Keep the information handy for the next step.

6. Reveal the stones to yourself. Match each bag to its crystal identity. Now open each package and take a look at the crystal.

7. Look at the information you intuitively picked up for each stone. Do you see a relationship between each stone's metaphysical properties and what you wrote down?

Here are selected impressions of a stone written
by a woman who did this exercise:

- Fluid, thick like honey: It's a good kind of thickness. Something with substance that can move.

- Soft, pale green: a color that is peaceful, calming, and nurturing.

- Outside looking in: an observer, observing.

- A cloud of green crossing my mind: A vision of a large tree in a meadow but up on a hill. A place where one can sit and read a book and look across green fields. I see a girl in a dress sitting with a book and a man that she likes. The image is like a movie or a story. It's very lovely.

- Movement like parting clouds. A peep-hole appearing. The moving clouds could possibly be in the previous scene.

- A peaceful feeling. Lying in the grass under a tree, springtime, temperature in the 70s, air is clean and slightly brisk: This is a familiar scene from my high school and college years. Both times, I had found a place in nature that became my "special" place. Although there was a bit of heartbreak at this time of my life, I was happy during those years. *(Wow! I didn't even realize this when I was writing the symbols above. I was just going one line at a time!!!)*

Complete Part 1 of exercise 5
before continuing to Part 2.

PART TWO

In one workshop I had someone who, while holding an unidentified stone, thought of a memory of being a young child, sitting outside with her father in the sunshine. In the memory, she was contented and happy, keeping herself amused as she was engaged in a childhood activity. When I revealed that the stone supported self-confidence and belief in oneself, she began choking up. She realized that within this memory she was without anxiety, doing something that was making her happy. This feeling of self-contentment created an energetic environment where her usual lack of self-confidence was unable to exist. The stone was reminding her that cultivating situations where she could feel engaged and contented naturally ameliorated any anxiety or lack of belief in herself.

It's information like this that you seek when intuitively connecting with a crystal. Your goal is to understand how the crystal can help and support you. You do this by intuitively connecting to the stone and discovering how that stone's energy interacts with yours. And like your personal symbols, what you pick up about the crystal will be the information that is most relevant to the energy of who you are.

Because I facilitate sessions as a crystal healer, I am able to see how the same stone affects a wide range of people. Thus I am in a position where I am better able to collate and summarize the global effects of a particular stone to share with the public. But unless you are specifically working with crystals to heal others, it's not important to know what a crystal does for someone else. Since you are your own main client, the information you need most is how the crystal works **for you**!

This is why intuitive impressions are so strongly related to your personal life and can come in the form of seemingly random memories. In the response to exercise 5 given opposite as an example, the person first got impressions of texture and color. These symbols then deepened into a scene that felt like a movie she was watching. She then realized the visions she had happened to pick up were actually a very personally compelling scene with her as the central character. Though each symbol she listed had been significant enough to be interpreted individually, every subsequent impression she wrote down revealed a deeper layer of meaning and insight connected with the stone. This allowed her to profoundly experience the specific tone of happiness that had been missing from her life and begin the journey of healing with this particular stone and connecting to this feeling once again.

233

OPPOSITE: Smoky Quartz   ABOVE: Pyrite ball

Green fluorite on quartz

"There is the music of Heaven in all things."

—Hildegard of Bingen

Determining the Authenticity of a Crystal's Metaphysical Description

Many metaphysical descriptions of crystals, like those found in books and online, have been paraphrased from another source. But each time a description becomes rephrased, the original meaning deteriorates. This unintentional outcome is often the result of a writer's attempt to communicate someone else's metaphysical information in their own words. If the writer does not have a true connection with the crystals, they will not have firsthand understanding to convey, and their resultant description will be a simulacrum—the surface appearance of what a crystal's properties are. It is as if Person A saw a movie and described it to Person B, and then Person B told you about the movie as though they had seen it themselves. Everything they would tell you about the characters, the emotions, the plot, and the way the movie looked would not be from their own experience but an interpretation of someone else's truth. In this same way, as the rephrasing of a crystal's metaphysical description continues from person to person, it breaks down even further into an oversimplified mess. This is why you find so many crystal descriptions with very basic statements like "balances your chakras," "guards against psychic attack," "transmutes energy," "promotes calm and peace," "helps with physical ailments," and other banal and overly generalized attributes. Lacking the potency of direct experience, the information, both distorted and watered down, no longer describes the true power of the crystals.

It also could be that the writer has firsthand experience but that what they pick up is not very deep. This is often a reflection of where the author is in their spiritual growth. If someone is spiritually wise, they will understand the karmic responsibility that comes with communicating metaphysical information and how important it is that this information comes from a place of service, integrity, and love. However, if what is being shared about the crystals is superficial, one has to question the motive of the author. If the author lacks experience and is a spiritual baby, they will not understand the gravity of the responsibility that comes with teaching spiritual information. They may not know how karmically important it is not to share misleading or inaccurate information. Another possible reason for the superficiality of their information could be that the writer wants to let others know how "spiritual" and "psychic" they are. Led by their egos, their metaphysical descriptions may bear little relation to the actual properties of the crystal itself and may instead be vaguely focused on the esoteric aspects of the crystal in a grandiose way.

One way to tell if a crystal description has been written by someone with a genuine relationship with the crystals is to see how specific their descriptions are. They will not write oversimplified explanations but will indicate in detail how the crystal is able to help you. The description should also relay how the crystal's properties help to heal some aspect of a core spiritual issue, rather than focus on material results that can be gained. Most importantly, the description should always convey, at least in an indirect or subtle way, an understanding and compassion for human beings and the human experience, so the tone of these descriptions will always be down to earth and grounded, with a feeling of love.

You also want to see if the message within the crystal description is consistent to a theme. If the description seems disjointed and randomly bounces across many subjects within a short space, I would question how deeply the author knows the crystal. The description should also help you clearly understand how the crystal specifically helps with some kind of soul issue. If the author has not precisely defined this, then depending on what they wrote, I would take what they have written lightly or not at all.

If the author has recommended artificial or enhanced crystals, you will also want to see if they are transparent about this fact and, if so, why they still recommend them. Although the recommendation of artificial and enhanced crystals is something I consider

Smoky Quartz

frightful, ultimately this book is about learning about your own intuition with the crystals and coming to your own conclusions about how crystal energies work with you.

Developing your intuitive abilities is less about being "right" than it is about learning how to gauge when something is energetically true to you. By comparing what you intuitively pick up with what someone else finds, you will get a sense of whose crystal information resonates with you the most. As you deepen your spiritual practice and become more aligned with your spiritual integrity, your intuitive recognition of what is spiritually real and true will become more sensitive and accurate, and whether or not someone is writing about crystals in a truly connected way will become more apparent.

Remember that your experience connecting to crystalline energy and understanding will be an ongoing journey without a finish line to cross. And it will take time to hone your spiritual radar so that you are able to discriminate between false and true teachings. So be gentle with yourself. No matter what you learn or how you learn it, you will always learn something, and it will contribute to your overall spiritual growth and healing.

CHAPTER 10

CLEANSING AND CHARGING YOUR CRYSTALS

BEFORE WE GET INTO THE DETAILS of the different kinds of metaphysical crystals and how you can use them to heal yourself, it's crucial to understand the importance of cleansing and charging your crystals.

Crystals by themselves are like ingredients in your pantry: It's not until you do something with them that the magic happens. It is only when you work with crystals with attention and gratitude that you allow your energy to collaborate with the energy given off by the stones. In this harmonic dance, your energy initiates a movement that the crystal can shape and form through its stable pattern of energy. The crystal feeds this renewed energy back to you, which you then accept, experience, and project as an evolved energy back to the crystal. Thus, in order to receive a crystal's energetic benefits, one must engage with it in a continual interactive relationship. If a person ignores this interaction, there will be no energy for the crystal to work with. This is the reason why someone can spend their whole life around crystals yet not experience any healing benefits from them. For although they share a physical space with crystals, they are not energetically working with them.

But even if you have been consciously interacting with a stone, after some time it may seem as though the crystal has stopped working. This is because, like a stuffed-up nose, your crystal has become energetically clogged up and has no space to continue working with your energies.

CLEANSING YOUR CRYSTALS

From a chemical standpoint, a solid is a substance whose chemical bonds hold atoms and molecules in a rigid shape. If this solid is specifically a crystalline solid, it means the atoms are held in a highly ordered structure in which billions of identical molecules are stacked upon each other in an orderly way, resulting in a crystal's overall shape.

But crystal building is not a perfect process. Occasionally in the crystal's lattice, atoms get substituted or sometimes go missing altogether. But these empty spaces within the crystalline lattice are precisely where the energy of your intention is held by the crystal!

In addition to the intention you put into the crystal, the crystal takes in energies from you. As you work together, your energy leaves artifacts within the spaces of the crystal, and over time the crystal can get clogged up with this old energetic information. As it runs out of space to transmute your energies, the crystal becomes energetically weighted down and can no longer do its job with ease. Just like a machine that has a lot of gunk jamming up the gears, a crystal will run more smoothly, powerfully, and efficiently when it is cleansed.

With all methods of crystal cleansing covered later in the chapter, **your intention to cleanse the crystal is an integral part of the process**. No matter the method, the physical act of cleansing is an empty motion without the intention to cleanse the stones, for it is the energy behind the intention that activates and catalyzes the cleansing process. This is why stones can be cleansed solely with pure thought. But because it takes a bit of Jedi-level training for your intention to be that clear and focused, it's far easier to cleanse stones in conjunction with a physical technique, for the movements within the physical task will help keep your intention focused on the stones.

THE DIFFERENCE BETWEEN CLEANSING AND CHARGING

Like getting your car washed versus filling it with gas, there is a difference between *cleansing* and *charging* crystals. *Cleansing* a crystal clears it of energetic debris, which allows the crystal to project its energies at its purest. When the crystal has been cleared of all other energies, it is at its most optimal state to have an intention put into it. *Charging* gives a crystal additional energy, allowing your crystal to work with more vibrancy and for a longer duration before it needs to be cleansed again. Charging can also increase the intensity of any intention placed into the stone.

While cleansing your crystals is absolutely necessary, charging your crystals is not—it is an optional process. However, if you *are* intending to charge your crystal, it's imperative to cleanse your crystal first so that any old energetic gunk does not get in the way of the intention you have set. Of these two practices, you will spend much more time cleansing than you will charging.

Some of the methods I describe below are purely cleansing or charging, but there are also methods that are a blend of both. Understand that these processes of cleansing and charging fall on a continuum, and much as the energies of crystals interact differently with you as an individual, so too do these cleansing and charging methods. To begin, you may find it's easier to use separate cleansing and charging methods (something I especially recommend for beginners) rather than methods that do both.

Each technique will align with the different elementals of earth, fire, air, and water—so depending on any astrological and/or natural energetic tendencies you have, you may find that certain types of cleansing or charging will be more suited to you than others. But it is only after you work with all the techniques that you will discover what you and your stones respond best to.

HOW TO CLEANSE AND CHARGE CRYSTALS

Leaving your crystals alone in a dark place for a long time will both cleanse and charge them. But since this process can take years, we need other ways to energetically cleanse and charge our frequently used stones.

There are numerous ways to cleanse and charge crystals, but the following are the core techniques to be familiar with. Though you are likely to have an affinity for certain techniques over others, you will still need to research each crystal you treat to make sure the method you use does not physically damage the stone.

Smudging

In addition to their medicinal healing properties, plants have vibrational qualities that can be used for energetic healing. One of the more familiar ways plants have been used energetically is through smudging—the ceremonial act of burning sacred plants. It's a method that invokes the use of the earth element (represented by the plant), the fire element (represented by the burning smoke), and the air element (where the smoke drifts through). Each smudge has a different energetic purpose and may be specifically used for cleansing, sanctifying, or welcoming good energies, or a combination of these purposes, depending on the specific energetic traits of the plant.

Sage, sweetgrass, palo santo, cedar, and juniper are some of the better-known sacred plants used for smudging. While these plants are easy to purchase as smudges, it is to your benefit to connect directly to the energies of a smudging plant by seeing it grow and move through its life cycle within the ecosystem it is a part of. This gives you a deeper understanding of the plant itself and leads to a better understanding of its energetic properties, while also further grounding and connecting you to the specific part of Mother Earth you live on.

So, if you are serious about using smudge and using it in a sacred way, learn about the sacred plants that grow in your area. You may not live near where the more popularly known smudges grow, but wherever you are there will be plants that can be used for smudging—they just may not be as well known.

If you want to learn about smudge and other sacred plants that grow around you, the best information will be found with the indigenous groups in your area who have worked, with deep honor and respect, with the plants that have been native to their land for generations. They, and the herbalists who have learned from them, are the greatest resource about a plant's medicine, both physical and energetic—and will also hold wisdom about the plant's life cycle and its place in the ecosystem. Learning this kind of information can make you more conscious of how to harness the plant's smudging energy so that it can be used in the most powerful way. Additionally, a responsible teacher will show you how to harvest the smudging plants that grow in your area in a sacred, respectful, and ethical way, with minimal impact to the plant and environment.

Smudging is a valuable tool because all things, including you and the crystals, have an auric field that can capture energies. Sometimes auric fields will capture negative energies, and the use of a cleansing smudge can help "unstick" these energies from these fields. A crystal's auric field will collect energies that will need to be cleared before the crystal can fully express its healing energies again. If you have a crystal that seems to have become "sluggish" and is not working so well anymore, it's likely that it is becoming bogged down by other unhelpful energies and needs to be cleansed. But you don't want to use just any kind of smudge to cleanse your crystal. You will specifically want to use what is called a *cleansing smudge* to clear the energies around your stone.

Of all cleansing smudges, sage is the most widely available and well known. But when it comes to smudges, *sage* is a bit of a catchall term, since it can include plants from either the Salvia or the Artemisia genus. However, it is the smudge from white sage, Salvia apiana, that is regarded as the most cleansing sage of all. This is the variety I most recommend to cleanse your crystals if you are not using a cleansing smudge plant native to your area.

When you cleanse your crystals, treat them like babies you are giving a bath. In the same way you wouldn't watch TV while absentmindedly bathing a baby, you do not want to be distracted while cleansing your crystal. Just as you would be present and focused when washing a baby, you need to be present and focused when cleansing a crystal. This means not being preoccupied with thinking about other things, such as what you need to do or a conversation you had earlier that day.

When you smudge, you don't need to create huge clouds of billowing smoke to cleanse your crystal (unless you want to trip your fire alarm). All the smoke you need can be produced from as little as one tiny leaf. As long as you can see and smell the smoke, it is enough to cleanse the stone.

To smudge, internally acknowledge the presence of the plant's energies and then gently circle the stone with the smoke. Imagine that you are giving the crystal a bath with the smoke. Have a clear intention that you are *cleansing* the stone so that any lingering negative energies that have been attached to the crystal's aura can now detach and allow the crystal to project its healing energies outward

Smoky quartz scepter,
cleansed by sage smudge

again. Remember, your presence and intention with the stone as you smudge make the process into a ceremony of respect. And it's the combination of your focused attention with the smudge's energies that produces the cleansing result.

One of the biggest benefits of using a cleansing smudge is that it can be used to cleanse all crystals. And because it works so well for clearing lingering energies, sage or any other cleansing smudge can be used to cleanse a crystal without losing any intention you may have previously set in it.

Water Cleansing

You can use water to cleanse your crystals physically, but did you know you can use water to energetically cleanse them as well? Water cleansing resonates with the water element, which rules emotions and the unconscious. Since so much of crystal healing involves processing these two aspects, water-based cleansing is an ideal way to cleanse crystals that have been energetically weighed down because of them.

Below are several different ways you can cleanse your crystals using different kinds of water.

SEA SALT AND WATER

Billions of years ago, our planet began as a ball of water. From the great watery expanse came single-celled life-forms that fed off the energy of the sun. From them, even more complex life-forms began to evolve to live on dry land. Dinosaurs gave way to mammalian life and then, over time, to us. Our species exists because of this lineage from our evolutionary oceanic ancestors who were birthed from Earth's waters, which cover approximately 71 percent of the crystal ball we call Earth. Of this water, 3.5 percent is freshwater, while the remaining 96.5 percent is salt water.

Salt water is the amniotic fluid of Earth. Even now, more than four billion years after the birth of our planet, ocean plankton begins the food web that weaves through every ecosystem on our planet, affecting every subsequent living being in the food chain. And all the water on this planet eventually flows back to the oceans, to be filtered and recycled again into new forms. So all life on this planet begins with Mother Earth's salty water, for it is the medium that holds her powerful energies of birth, nourishment, and renewal.

"There must be something
strangely sacred in salt. It is in our
tears and in the sea."
–Khalil Gibran, *Sand and Foam*

Crystals cleansed in water sprinkled with
sea salt. Clockwise from top left: petrified
wood, quartz, apatite, dalmatian stone

To cleanse a crystal using this potent method, all you need to do is to submerge a crystal in water that has been sprinkled with sea salt. For routine cleansing, let the crystal sit in this bath for at least twenty minutes. If the crystal needs a more thorough cleansing, keep it in this solution overnight or longer, until it feels cleansed.

Though it is not as powerful as the living water method described below, the sea salt and water method is powerful and works relatively quickly, and, because of this, is the cleansing method I recommend the most.

TAP WATER

While sea salt and water is my favorite way to cleanse crystals, if you are in a situation where your crystal needs to be cleansed but you are not in a place or do not have the time for other, more deeply cleansing methods, simply placing your crystal under running tap water will give it a quick and temporary cleanse.

There are times when you are going to be working very intensely with a stone and will have little time to cleanse it. This happens most often with stones you work with every day, like pocket stones, or stones whose persons are dealing with a lot of negative energies, like black tourmaline. Though you will eventually need to cleanse your crystal with a method that cleanses it more deeply, by rinsing the crystal under tap water you will keep the stone's energy going for another day or so.

LIVING WATER

The most powerful method of water cleansing involves the use of living water from nature. Any water that comes directly from Mother Earth—like a clear running stream, a pocket of seawater left in a tide pool, gently lapping waves on a lake, water flowing out of a natural hot spring, or rain coming down from the sky—has her energetic signature written on it. Because it is created by, and comes directly out of, the vibrant, living body of Mother Earth, it is considered *living water* and carries Mother Earth's water-healing energies at her purest and most powerful.

Living water will both cleanse and charge crystals. If you place your crystals in a body of Mother Earth's water, the freshness of her energy combined with the movement of her water will cleanse the stones, while her undiluted energies will charge them. Because of how powerful her energies are, the crystals will quickly be both cleansed and charged, most of the time intensely so within just a few minutes.

A couple of caveats: First, if the water is polluted, don't use it for cleansing your crystals—it won't have the energies you're looking for. Second, don't contain the water (meaning, don't scoop up the water into a bucket or some other container and place the crystals inside)—you want the water to remain connected to the Earth. This may mean placing the crystals in a shallow crevice or holding your crystals as the water runs over them. Be careful, though—sometimes the crystals are so excited about feeling Mother Earth's healing energy in this way again that they are compelled to leap from your hands, back into the water where they will return to their cozy womb in Mother Earth. So pay attention to where you choose to place or hold your crystals when using this method, because you may potentially become separated from them. But if you do and are unable to find the crystals again, do not be upset. Though you may have paid for them and cared for them, they have always been on loan from Mother Earth, so if they should choose to return back to her, release them freely with love and gratitude.

PRECAUTIONS

Not all crystals are physically compatible with water cleansing because some crystals will dissolve in water. Halite, for example, is literally naturally crystallized salt and thus will dissolve completely in water. Other minerals, like selenite, may not dissolve as quickly but will become permanently dulled if left in water for too long. Even if the crystal itself is not water soluble, if it is in the form of a mineral specimen it may still be susceptible to coming apart at the joins where the different individual crystals come together. So it is imperative to research if your individual stones can be water cleansed if you want to keep them intact. And if you are in doubt, choose another, non-water-based method.

Selenite

In the world of metaphysical crystals, selenite is used to describe all forms of the mineral gypsum—from clear to fibrous and from colorless to tinted. While some varieties of selenite have color, for the purposes of cleansing crystals you want to use the untinted variety that is either clear or translucent white.

OPPOSITE: This beautiful and rare halite should
not be cleansed by water, because the crystal
will completely dissolve: its chemical formula is
NaCl–also known as salt!

ABOVE: A selenite rod cleansing
some brochantite

What's special about selenite is that it doesn't need to be cleansed. Selenite continually channels large amounts of high-vibration divine energy through itself, and this keeps the stone naturally cleansed. This movement of energy is so constant and powerful that in addition to cleansing itself, selenite can energetically cleanse other stones too!

To cleanse with selenite, place the crystals to be cleansed very close to or touching the selenite as shown in the photo on the previous page. Leave them next to the selenite, in sunlight if possible, for a day or more, depending on how much cleansing the crystals need. Like sage, selenite is a great way to cleanse all stones. The larger the selenite is, the more effective it will be for cleansing, so opt for a large specimen if you are getting a selenite specifically for this purpose.

Moonlight

People often tell me that they wait for the full moon to cleanse their crystals. Although placing stones in moonlight is a method of cleansing them and a beautiful way to ritually connect with moon energies, if you're waiting about once a month for the full moon you are probably not cleansing your heavily used stones frequently enough. Crystals you are using intensely (which is often the case with stones like hematite and black tourmaline) will require more frequent cleansing, sometimes even daily, to work optimally, so cleansing once a month is not enough.

In comparison to other cleansing methods, the energy of moonlight is very gentle, which makes it ideal for cleansing stones that have gentle energies too. It's also a great method to use for crystals whose color would otherwise fade and/or permanently change when exposed to light.

Most crystals that are sensitive to light are pale-colored and transparent, though even a dark-hued crystal like amethyst can fade in bright light. In the case of amethyst, exposure to light slowly changes the crystal from purple to colorless, a shift that changes the chakra the crystal resonates with. So if you have chosen a crystal specifically for the chakra it works with, you are likely to want to cleanse it with methods that keep its color intact, like moon cleansing.

Rather than using moonlight for cleansing, I prefer to work with moon energies as a way to charge stones and give them a soft and gentle boost of feminine energy.

This amethyst was cut in half and one side was put in the sunlight. Because amethyst is light-sensitive, after a year of exposure, the right-hand side lost virtually all its color.

Moonlight energies work well for facilitating transitions, like breakups or moving from one home to another, or for situations where introspection and quiet inward understanding would be helpful. In these cases, I would use moonlight energy to charge my stones.

Each phase of the moon brings different energies to the cleansing and charging of your crystals, so if you're going to be working with moon energies it is important to learn about the respective energies each of the different phases brings. In brief, the full moon brings waning energy, which is an energy of release as the full moon shrinks into the blackness of the new moon. The new moon (when the moon cannot be seen and is at the beginning of its journey to enlarge into a full moon) brings an energy of growth. Each phase's energies can be then used to enhance (or charge) the intention you put into your crystal.

Sunlight

In contrast to the gentle, soft, and feminine energy of moonlight, sunlight is the masculine counterpart of celestial light energy. Sunlight energy is strong and vibrant. Its energy feeds, strengthens, and moves forward. This makes sunlight's masculine energy ideal for charging stones. As long as your crystal is not sensitive to light

HOW OFTEN DO
I CLEANSE MY CRYSTALS?

Q: *Now that I know how to cleanse, how often do I cleanse my crystals?*
A: **On an as-needed basis.**

In our modern world, we gravitate toward prescriptions. Because we are busy or perhaps a little lazy, we want someone else to tell us how to do things so we don't have to think about them. But to develop your skills with crystals, you have to discover how they work for yourself. Rather than relying on me to tell you that you need to cleanse your crystals once a week or once a month, you need to get to a place where you intimately understand when a crystal needs to be cleansed. After all, you are deepening your relationship with the crystals by learning to make one-on-one connections with them, so learning how to listen to them is essential for your crystal intuitive development.

Let me put it this way:

Q: *How many times should you pee?*
A: **On an as-needed basis.**
   You pee when you need to go. If you drink a lot of water, you'll need to go more frequently.

Q: *When should you wash your dishes?*
A: **On an as-needed basis.**
   Maybe you'll wait until you've run out of dishes, or maybe you want to do it more frequently because you want a clean, tidy kitchen.

Q: *So when do you cleanse your crystals?*
A: **On an as-needed basis!**

My favorite story about when to cleanse crystals happened with a client who had a young child with recurring bad nightmares. I recommended to the mother that she place a black tourmaline underneath her child's pillow. Months later, when browsing social media, I saw she had posted a photo of herself at the breakfast table doing crafts with her daughter. In the caption the mother wrote that her daughter had begun having nightmares again, but she realized she hadn't cleansed the black tourmaline underneath her daughter's pillow recently, so she cleansed the stone. For the next couple nights, her daughter had slept so soundly that early that next morning they were able to do crafts!

Cleanse stones when they need to be cleansed. If you're using a stone intensely, you'll need to cleanse it more frequently. That may mean once every three weeks, once every three days, or every day, depending on how much you are leaning on the stone and how much the stone can energetically handle. The easiest way to figure out if your stone needs to be cleansed is to ask yourself:

1. Does the stone seem like it has stopped working?
2. When was the last time I cleansed the stone?

As in the case of the mother and child, if your stone has stopped working it's likely because it needs to be cleansed. If you're in doubt, just cleanse it. If after thoroughly cleansing your stone you still feel as though it is no longer helping you, it may mean you need the energies of a different stone altogether. The only way to know is to experiment. Any experience you have will benefit the development of your intuition with the crystals. So get out all your crystals, cleanse them, and see what happens!

Amethyst

CHAPTER 11

THE DIFFERENT KINDS OF METAPHYSICAL CRYSTALS

NOW THAT YOU HAVE COMPLETED the exercises, you are able to recognize your natural intuitive abilities with the crystals. Because you have a better understanding of how the crystals resonate with your energy, you are able to pick out helpful stones to work with. But before you begin to work with the stones, you must learn the differences between the major categories of metaphysical crystals. The following is a breakdown of the primary kinds of metaphysical stones you will encounter and the advantages of each.

POCKET STONES

The ubiquitous pocket stone can be found in every metaphysical shop. A category consisting of tumbled stones, unfinished rough rocks, and small crystal points, pocket stones are so named because they easily fit in your pocket.

Pocket stones are an important part of your crystal tool kit. Because they are both easy to obtain and portable, they are the type of crystals you are most likely to work with. And though pocket stones can range in price from very inexpensive to very expensive depending on how common or rare they are, they are still the most economical type of metaphysical crystal.

They also tend to be sturdy enough for the rougher handling that happens in day-to-day life. Many pocket stones, especially the ones in tumbled form, can withstand the rigors of being kept in your pocket and bumping against your keys without getting damaged. Because of this hardiness, they can be used in situations where you don't want to worry about how the crystals are being handled. This makes pocket stones fundamental to your crystal tool kit.

Because you will likely use your pocket stones frequently, they will need to be cleansed frequently as well. However, the effort needed to cleanse pocket stones will always be minimal compared to the benefits you can reap from them energetically.

MINERAL SPECIMENS

Mineral specimens are unadulterated crystals in their original form as they were created by Mother Earth. Because they express her energy in the purest form, these kinds of crystals are the most powerful of all types of metaphysical crystals. This is why these crystals are the type I most encourage crystal seekers to interact with, as they hold the most potent form of crystalline energy.

However, most metaphysical shops favor carrying pocket stones or other cut and polished mineral pieces because these are the crystals most often featured in crystal reference books. Virtually all of the crystal and metaphysical shops I have been to depend on the descriptions written in books like these to explain the properties of the crystals they carry. And their customers are dependent on these texts too. There is a tendency for people to want crystals most when something becomes pressing in their lives. In their urgency to seek crystalline support, they refer to crystal books or information they have found online to find the crystal that matches what they believe their issue to be. Once they find a description that seems most pertinent to their issue, they become quite single-minded about getting this particular crystal, for they have a mistaken belief that only this precise crystal can solve their problem. And even if they haven't done any research before going into the crystal shop, I still notice people spending more time reading the metaphysical description written on a stone's placard (most likely referenced from a crystal book) than looking at the stones themselves.

Another reason that shops are less likely to carry raw mineral specimens is that they cannot be easily categorized the way pocket stones are. Pocket stones come from mines that produce such vast quantities of a single mineral that it's possible to widely distribute them. As will be explained further in "The Economics of Rare shows to see just how vast and beautiful the crystalline world is beyond the pages of any crystal reference book or the images that appear in a Google search. And more importantly, these shows give you the firsthand opportunity to tune in to your crystal intuitive abilities on a wide variety of stones.

Shopping for Mineral Specimens

Crystal shops sometimes sell mineral specimens, but when they do I find they tend to sell specimens of lower quality. This is because quality mineral specimens are significantly pricier than pocket stones, and most people tend to want to buy the cheapest thing that gets the job done. If you seek quality mineral specimens, you generally have to go outside of metaphysical shops and seek out dealers who are dedicated to the scientific side of minerals and mineral collecting.

Like any collecting genre, mineral collecting is filled with all different kinds of collecting nerds. Dealers often specialize their offerings and may focus on selling minerals from a certain country, minerals with certain attributes (fossils, fluorescence, microcrystals), minerals from a particular mineral family, and so on. Also, each dealer's stock tends to focus at a price point that appeals to a certain type of mineral collector—from stones that fit a young mineral hobbyist's allowance all the way to million-dollar specimens bought by museums and high-end collectors.

Dealers frequently have come to mineral dealing because of their backgrounds in physical science. Many have degrees in geology or chemistry, are often charmingly full of intriguing tidbits about minerals, and will not hesitate to enthusiastically share their excitement about their passion with you. They are truly a wealth of scientific information about crystals. However, if you ask them about the *metaphysical* properties of a crystal, they won't have any information. In fact, you're likely to get a real queer look from them. Being of decidedly scientific mind, they do not find merit in metaphysics and view metaphysical crystal collectors as kooks. But they are quite polite about it, for we share with them a passionate love of rocks. (And it also probably helps that we kooks are often a significant portion of their business and so they find it unnecessary to offend an important customer base.)

CUT AND POLISHED STONES

Before it becomes a cabochon, crystal pyramid, sphere, or polished slab, each stone begins as an unassuming hunk of rough rock. But in order to bring out the stone's color and texture, it has to be cut and polished. This allows you to see its beauty, which helps you form a stronger connection to the energies of the stone.

Chapter 6 (page 167) explained the potential pitfalls that are related to cut and polished stones. But as a quick recap, remember that it is imperative that any cut and polished stone has been created for a valid metaphysical purpose that helps the stone's energy be harnessed and enhanced. If you are considering purchasing any kind of cut and polished stone, including jewelry that contains cabochons or gemstones, carefully weigh the information presented in that chapter to help determine if the stone you are considering is worthy of investment.

Also, be conscientious about the reasons why you choose a certain cut and polished stone over getting it in its raw form. For raw stones are powerful too, and even something as humble as a chunk of unpolished rose quartz can have the ability to profoundly heal you as well as fill you with immense happiness and delight.

From left to right: Pyritized ammonite, skeletal
pyrite, pyrite river stone, cubic pyrite in matrix

The Economics of
Rare Crystals

Though their chemical formulas can be exactly the same, variables of temperature, pressure, and time create ultraspecific geological conditions that cause minerals from one part of the world to have a different shape than the same minerals found in another part of the world (that is, to differ in what geologists call their "crystal habit"). So even minerals with the same chemical formula can potentially be found as spheres, cubes, or octahedrons depending on where they come from. These nuances in shape are valuable both to scientifically minded collectors and metaphysical crystal buyers. While most mineral collectors are interested in rarity, the nuances in energy are significant enough to lead metaphysical collectors to choose one shape over another.

For instance, pyrite is a mineral that expresses itself into many different final forms. While all forms of pyrite deal with the energy of taking ephemeral ideas and manifesting them into an embodied physical form, each iteration of pyrite adjusts this energy for a different effect. The most commonly seen form of pyrite exhibits itself as a profuse cluster of complex crystal faces. This kind of pyrite is best for someone who wants to manifest many different smaller ideas without a structured final result. In contrast, cubic pyrite takes a form that is one of the most stable shapes when placed on flat ground—the cube—making this crystal ideal for someone who wants to manifest something physical that has a discrete physical beginning and ending (and likely a firm finish date), like a term paper or the construction of a building. Spherical pyrite is chemically built in layers, with the sphere getting larger as more mineral is added to its exterior. This makes it a good form of pyrite for someone who is working on a project that has an indefinite end date or for someone with projects that need to continue to develop and grow over time, like the evolving manifestation of an artist's oeuvre or the building of a company or business. These are just a few of the varieties of pyrite, and though they all deal with manifestation into the physical, their nuances in form lead to significant differences in how their energy is projected.

As new and different forms of minerals are discovered and enter the market, people begin working with these crystals and writing about their specific metaphysical properties. But by the time their book is published with these stones' specific metaphysical information, the supply of stones may have already dried up. This is because there is no way to predict how much supply of a crystal exists. Since minerals are found underground, it is impossible to know exactly how much of a mineral there is. Sometimes a mineral pocket can last a few years, or perhaps even decades, before the mine becomes exhausted. Sometimes only a single small pocket of minerals is ever discovered. Sometimes the supply stops because the mineral pocket has collapsed and has become unreachable or too dangerous to explore. And sometimes mine owners find that they can make a bigger profit by closing off the mine and paving it over to build a hotel or an airport runway. Because of all these factors, the supply of a specific crystal can suddenly become limited, and like any other collectable the stone will become rare. At the same time, the publicity the crystal has since received in books and media will cause it to become well known and coveted. Thus demand rises against a limited supply, and the price of the crystal naturally goes up to what the market can bear.

This is why it's so helpful to develop your own personal intuitive connection to the crystals. As in cooking, when you can substitute an ingredient in a recipe, you are able to discover new, previously unpublished or underrated stones that work even better than ones you might have read about. So developing your intuition with crystals gives you the freedom to go into any rock shop and choose a stone that works for you, simply because you are able to connect directly to its energy and understand what the stone is about. No longer are you bound to the vagaries of mineral economics or the dictates of any "crystal experts." Instead, you are self-empowered, able to decide for yourself what is metaphysically important to you—or not!

OPPOSITE: Amethyst with prehnite

ABOVE: The staggered growth of this tectonic quartz is caused by thin intermittent layers of calcite interrupting the quartz's growth.

Polyhedral Agate

Jacinto Quartzes

This tabular quartz specimen is about
19 centimeters high but amazingly is
only 1.6 centimeters thick.

This quartz intergrew with another unknown
mineral that later dissolved away, leaving it
with this deeply etched surface.

"Don't try to comprehend with your mind.
Your minds are very limited. Use your intuition."
—Madeleine L'Engle, *A Wind in the Door*

ABOVE: Green tourmaline in quartz

OPPOSITE: Some may not consider this smoky quartz "pretty." But notice the fissure: it's where the crystal was broken but began growing again over the fractured area. This is what is geologically known as a self-healed or re-healed crystal. Does knowing its persistence make the crystal prettier to you?

Selenite star upon a mini altar alongside sage

Take a deep breath, close your eyes, and then exhale. Then imagine *applying* the energy of the crystal on you. You can imagine the energy of the crystal being transmitted to you, or you can literally sweep the air around the crystal over your head and down your back, distributing the crystal's energy on yourself. This ceremony attunes you to the crystal, which helps you carry the energy of the crystal with you throughout your day. Just like applying your lipstick or fixing your hair before you step away from the mirror, this action becomes part of your daily grooming routine, preparing you for your day.

At the end of your day as you get ready to go to bed, check in with your crystal again. Notice if the crystal's energy has helped you by recollecting if there was any change in how you interacted with your life that day. And again, *apply* the energy of the crystal on you before you go to sleep.

Doing this practice every day embosses the stone's energy into you. And each day you continue to do this ceremony further embosses the energy into your energetic body. As you become even more connected to the crystal, you will better notice and feel its healing effects. You will begin to see that the crystal is more than a tool for healing. You will begin to feel how your crystal cares for you as you feel its energy supporting and working with you. You will begin to realize that the crystal is your *friend*.

Continue using your crystal as your altar stone until you have reached a desired result or until you intuitively feel the need to take a break, then put the crystal aside. However, this does not necessarily mean that you are finished working with the stone. In fact, most of the time it doesn't. After working with a crystal for some time and resolving a layer of energetic patterning, you may find there are other energetic patterns that have taken front stage and that need more attention to be resolved. At that point, you would change the crystal you've been working with for another crystal that better matches the metaphysical support you then need. After working to heal those patterns, you may find that the next layer of patterning needing to be worked on is a deeper iteration of the energies you previously worked on. At that point, you would return to the crystal you worked with before.

As you go through your life, you will find that it continually touches upon certain themes. These are the themes that you, as a soul, have decided to extensively explore in this lifetime. Perhaps one these themes is learning to loudly and boldly

speak up for yourself, or being more vulnerable and open, or understanding the responsibility that comes with having power. These themes may simply appear to be recurring problems you have with your life, but the reason they show up again and again is to help you to gain proficiency with the energies that are contained within the theme. Thus it's never exactly the same situation twice, for each scenario gives you the opportunity to experience a different iteration, aspect, or deeper lesson of how the dynamics of the energy within each theme work.

This is also why you will find yourself returning to the same stone again and again as you continue with your healing journey. Though you may work with many other crystals, you will have certain core crystals whose energies will help you the most. Thus, recognizing when you need to work with a particular crystal again is part of your learning process with the crystals. Over time, with experience, you will understand when it is the right time to work with a crystal again.

OTHER SIGNIFICANT SPACES

In addition to altar spaces, you can put crystals in any space that belongs to you for energetic support.

If you have a crystal you want to work with in this way, think about what the crystal metaphysically supports and then place it in an area where its energy can best help. For instance, pyrite is helpful for getting projects manifested and completed into the physical dimension. It also has the benefit of grounding disruptive subtle electromagnetic energies coming from electronics. Pyrite is therefore an ideal candidate to be placed at your desk, by your computer, for if you are working at a desk with a computer, it's likely you are in the process of getting some sort of project manifested and completed!

You can also approach this the other way around: If you have a space that needs a certain kind of energy, figure out what it is that you want to achieve, and then find a crystal to support it. For instance, if there have been disagreements within the home and you would like to shift them into harmony, you can bring black tourmaline in to help recycle the negative energy into positive energy. You may want to place the black tourmaline where family members spend the most time

together—for instance, at the dining table or upon a shelf where it can be seen by the whole family. Or perhaps you will place it in the living room, where the family gets together to watch TV. The important point is to place the crystal where the energetic issue most often happens.

One of my favorite stories regarding crystal placement is from one of my workshops. A mother asked if her bedroom was a good place for a citrine crystal. Since citrine is about manifestation, I asked if she wanted to have more children. Her eyes widened and a look of horror crossed her face as she tried to imagine fitting another child into her already busy life. She immediately and emphatically shook her head no while the class smiled and laughed. The bedroom, she realized, was the last place she wanted manifesting energy. But she did have some work projects she was hoping to manifest, so I suggested she place the citrine somewhere in her office, as it was a better place for the crystal's energy to be to help her toward her goals.

When determining the best space for a crystal to go, think symbolically. Because each room has particular activities associated with it, each room will cultivate certain energies. A living room can be a place for socialization, while an entryway is a place for welcoming or sending off energies. Perhaps you want your child's room to support nurturing and safety, or fun and growth. Crystals can be placed in each location to support the energies of that particular space. If you try this and discover the crystal does not give you the kind of support you need, you can always move it somewhere else and try another one in its place. Again, a lot about working with crystals is experimenting and seeing what happens. It's like trying out a new ingredient when cooking: You can read every book and article you can get your hands on and research a hundred recipes using the ingredient, yet nothing will replace what you will learn just by cooking with it. It's the same way with crystals.

Make the placement of the crystal a ceremony. Use some smudge, share your intention with your crystal, and thank it for helping you. Check in on the crystal and keep it regularly cleansed. Your attention will help it to understand where its energy needs to go and keep it working optimally to support you.

CRYSTAL GRIDS

The practice of putting crystals in significant spaces, sanctifying them, reenergizing them, and then taking note of their results is important to understand if you want to work with crystals in crystal grids. Crystal grids can be powerful tools to harness the energies of different stones working in conjunction with each other to affect a space or situation. However, you do need to have some experience before you can work with them effectively.

With the resurgence of interest in crystals, I have seen many photos, especially on social media, of crystal grids. Unfortunately, many of these grids are simply stones put into pretty patterns without much thought given to what each of the stones' energies do and how they work together. This is why I encourage you to repeatedly practice working with the same crystal so that you understand it energetically inside and out. Arranging a bunch of crystals together without understanding their properties is the energetic equivalent of cooking random ingredients together and expecting to make a delicious meal. Even if you arranged your ingredients prettily on the plate, it still wouldn't mean what you made would be tasty to eat.

When cooking, knowing how individual ingredients work helps you to create a better meal on the whole. You understand which flavors can work together and in what ratios they work together best. In the same way, working with crystals individually helps you understand which crystals have the potential to work well together and in what proportion you want their energies in order to get the result you seek.

Like all crystal work, which crystal grids work best for you is dependent on what your energy responds to, and you'll learn this only by working with the crystals in a diligent and patient way. Until then, you will get a lot of benefit working with crystals individually, and though they may not look anything like the overly ornate ones you see online, you'll naturally begin to find yourself making crystal grids.

CRYSTAL HEALING FOR OTHERS

This book is meant to be a beginner's guide for working with crystals. It has been structured to help you build a strong foundation in working with crystalline energies so that you may bring strength and healing into your life. But as you begin to benefit from the crystals and experience the profound healing they can bring, you'll naturally want to help others, especially the people you love. The more you work with the crystals, the more you will understand their potential to bring strength and support to those who have been struggling and suffering. You will want to help others, for you will be able to see hope where others have none.

However, as you journey on your own path of spiritual development and healing, you will learn the importance of not impinging on other people's energetic space. To ignore this is in direct violation of spiritual law.

This is the guideline: **Do not send energies to anyone without their permission.**

I cannot stress how important this is. You wouldn't want someone to barge unannounced and without permission into your home and start rearranging your belongings, throwing out all the things they think you don't need and putting stuff you don't want in their place. This would be a violation of you and your space. It would demonstrate a lack of respect for you, your decisions, and how you choose to live your life.

In the same way, everyone has an energetic space. How they live within that space is their own choice. Even if it's starkly clear that someone is damaging their own life with the decisions they make or what they do to their body, it is not up to you to change it for them. You must let them live their life. Even if they are on a path of self-destruction, you have to let them go there. This is spiritual law. It is not your journey to take; nor is it your choice to make.

As well-intentioned as you may be, you can't be sure that you'll be able to make the best decisions for someone else. Heck, you probably have challenges making the best decisions for yourself. So when it comes to any form of energetic healing, including crystal healing, you must not send any healing energy to anyone else *unless you have their explicit permission to do so*. If you send them healing without it, I guarantee it will

backfire. Out of resistance, the person you want to heal will not get the healing, and you'll get karmically scorched too.

The only exception to these guidelines is if you are a parent or guardian to a child or someone who is fully dependent on you. When a child is young, they are under your care and you are responsible for guiding them in all matters of life. They do not yet have the capacity to accurately weigh certain kinds of decisions. And though young children may be more open to your spiritual help, as they get older you may encounter resistance from them. It's very important not to force any energetic healing on them, for they need their own space to discover what is spiritually right for themselves. If you force healing on them, it will give them a negative experience and a bad taste in their mouth that only serves to make them resist any kind of healing energy now and into their future. But if you allow them to discover the healing energies in their own way, you actually promote the chance for them to heal, for you have given them the energetic space to explore the potential of these energies.

If a teenager or an adult declines crystals or crystalline energy, be respectful of their wishes. Like attempting to give tasty food to someone who doesn't want to try it, it's pointless to bring healing energy to someone if they don't want to accept it. Forcing them to interact with any energy will cause them to doubly resist and further condition them to respond negatively to the healing energy.

But if they look at you incredulously and say, "This is stupid," "What a joke," or "You're crazy," but say, "Yes" to accepting the crystal, then you are karmically in the clear. By saying "Yes" or "Okay," even with a tone of derision, they have offered consent. Despite any outer skepticism, something inside of them is allowing for just a little opening of healing to come in and help them.

If you wish to bring crystal healing to your loved ones, you can give them a crystal or stone that you feel would support them. You can share what techniques have worked for you, give them some simple instructions on what they can do with the crystal, or even encourage them to read this book. But don't expect they will be as enthusiastic as you are about the crystals. Although they may show interest, they may not be ready to fully commit to the healing work involved and may not do

anything with the crystal you give them. This is fine. When they are ready, they will interact with the stone. Don't put any expectations on them, and give them the space to come around on their own. Though your intent is to help them become healed specifically with crystalline energy, your patience itself is an act of healing love.

Though laying crystals on someone's body doesn't seem to be a very big deal, since it appears quite gentle, beautiful, and serene, the actual experience of having many crystal energies interact with one's energy is far more dramatic. While it's one thing to place crystals on your own body, laying crystals on others means that you are using crystals to actively affect someone else's energies. You are causing the person's energy to react to the crystalline energy and open up deeper, more complicated layers of themselves all the way to their soul. This process reveals all the icky energetic stuff that has been holding a person back, and to complete the process you are required to guide them through very intense places that wouldn't necessarily be defined as "fun." In fact, these places can be quite scary, so if you are intending to perform this kind of healing you have to make sure you are fully prepared to encounter these energies and not be scared by them, while making sure the person you are helping is fully protected too. So laying crystals on a person's body is not something you do in a casual or flippant way for "fun." In the same way that you wouldn't perform major surgery without years of medical training, you wouldn't facilitate the more powerful forms of crystal healing without extensive training. While people recognize how complicated surgery can be, many people don't understand the seriousness of energy healing and just how delicate, complicated, and grave it actually is.

Unskilled or misguided people trying to work with crystals in this way can easily harm others with their incompetence, causing damage both to the person having their energies worked on and to themselves. Not only will the person wanting to be healed be harmed, but also the person attempting to facilitate the healing then must carry the energy of their mistakes until they take responsibility for their ignorance and repair the damage they have done. So, until you have training and experience in laying crystals on others, you want to avoid doing this kind of healing. Either get training (there are resources for crystal healing training listed in the back of the book) or practice only on yourself until you do. If you don't want to go through

training and still want to lay crystals on someone other than yourself, just be aware that you will face the repercussions of any harm you've caused, even if your intent was innocent or the result accidental.

If you want to help others with crystal healing, a powerful way to do it is to share your experiences of the crystals with them and teach them what you know. Honestly answering their questions is one of the best ways you can help others understand and develop their own relationship with the crystals. However, if you want to know the most powerful way you can help others with crystalline energy, *I'll let you in on a secret*: The most powerful thing you can do to help a loved one—more powerful than giving them a crystal or sending them healing energy—is to shift your own energy.

As you heal, your energy changes, and a ripple effect is created where the dynamic of every relationship you are connected to automatically shifts in response. Every relationship you have will change to some degree, and all for the better. In my own experience I have seen acrimonious relationships dissolve instantly into love through the powerful healing energy of the crystals. I've seen whole families heal just because one person shifted and healed their own energy. I've seen people suddenly find their life partner shortly after they find themselves. In my metaphysical history I've seen some pretty wild things, but I'm still astounded by the crazy miracles that happen as the result of someone healing themselves first.

So don't worry about giving crystals or healing energy to those who don't want it. Focus on your own deep healing and you will find that the energy of others will naturally change around you.

Cubic Pyrite

ALTAR SPACES

When crystals and mineral specimens are too delicate or large to be carried around, creating an altar space for them is an excellent way to help direct their healing energies toward you.

Through my crystal intuitive readings, I have discovered that crystals often want to be placed wherever their people get ready for the day. Frequently, this means in the bathroom, on the dresser, or in any other area where a person spends time grooming and giving attention to themselves. If you want to try this approach, choose a crystal with metaphysical properties related to what you would like help with. Place the crystal in your preferred "special" area. This may be in a corner, on a shelf, or in any other place that feels a touch more exalted. You may wish to feature the crystal in a way that makes it stand out from the objects around it, for example in a bowl or on a raised pedestal. Next, write down on a piece of paper what you would like the crystal to help you with. As explained in exercise 3 (page 134), the most important thing is to capture the *feeling* of the result you are seeking rather than a specific outcome. For example, if you're working with a crystal to help you have a better relationship with yourself, you could write down, "*Crystal, please help me to feel nurtured and cared for. Help me to understand how to have strong boundaries and not overextend myself to others in spite of myself. Help me to love myself so I can find joy and happiness without feeling guilt about taking care of myself.*"

Then do a ceremony with your crystal. Smudge your crystal with sacred smoke and have the intention of cleansing the crystal and sanctifying the ceremony. Hold the crystal, close your eyes, and ask the crystal to please partner with you to support you in your journey of healing. Transmit the feelings and intentions you wrote in your note to the crystal so it can energetically understand what you would like its help for. Hold the crystal until you feel a subtle bonding connecting you to the crystal. If you don't sense this, simply hold the crystal until you feel you have clearly and succinctly communicated your feelings. Then thank the crystal and place it on top of your note in its special spot.

Every morning take a moment to be present with your crystal. Touch and/or look deeply at your crystal and reiterate what you wish the crystal to help you with.

WAYS TO WORK
WITH CRYSTALS

CHAPTER 13

HOW TO CHOOSE METAPHYSICAL CRYSTALS

YOU PICKED UP THIS BOOK because you desired to understand the power of crystals. Somehow, you have always known there was something to them, that they were more than just rocks, that they were indeed powerful and had great capacity to heal. But though you sensed all these things, you didn't know how to recognize and feel their energies, so the idea of a crystal having healing powers often felt like a fantasy—something you wanted to believe in, but something you weren't sure was even true. Yet even with all your doubts you still felt connected to them.

So you began reading this book, hoping that it would give you the answers you had been seeking. But as you read through the chapters, you discovered that this book did not have simple, straightforward answers or easy formulas you could thoughtlessly follow—nothing was clear-cut. Though you live in a world filled with flashy graphics, brief summaries, video clips, and other forms of informational instant gratification, this book asked you to shift gears and immerse yourself into a slower and more careful way of learning.

The exercises in this book have implored you to carefully and diligently comb through the details of crystalline understanding, and because of this thorough process you have been able to see that your hunches about crystalline energy were indeed accurate and that you did have a connection with the crystals that was real. You experienced that sensing and understanding crystalline energies was not an ability reserved for the select and gifted few but one that everyone has. But in order to get to this point, you needed a more thorough understanding of metaphysics and, more importantly, a more thorough understanding of yourself.

My purpose in writing this book was to help you understand and work with crystals in a way that truly empowered and healed you. Because you have taken the time to read through the chapters, complete the exercises, and expand your own intuitive capabilities, you now have a deeper understanding of the crystals.

You now know why stones conscientiously taken out of the Earth are in better condition both physically and energetically, and why they are pricier than other crystals that are more easily found in most stores. But you are also aware that while rare stones are more coveted, it's actually the commonly available stones that are most energetically useful and needed. And you have learned about the different kinds of metaphysical crystals that are available and how you can work with them.

Now that you have all the necessary information to understand the nuances in stones, we can move on to how to choose your crystals.

WORK WITH CRYSTALS INDIVIDUALLY AND TAKE YOUR TIME WITH THEM

I know what it's like to walk into a crystal shop and not want to leave without bringing a dozen crystals home. But buying many crystals at once is just like bringing home a large haul of clothing: Though you'll add many new items to your closet, you'll find that you wear only a few pieces regularly. Months later, when you look in your closet and see all the clothing you forgot you had, you will find that you are no longer in the mood to wear it anymore.

This same experience can happen when you are buying many crystals at once. After bringing them home, you will find that you will gravitate to one of them, and the rest will get put away with others you previously bought. Or you might bring many crystals home and work with them in a sporadic way, switching between them when nothing seems to be happening. You'll keep bouncing from crystal to crystal, maybe even going back to the shop to buy more, because you still aren't getting the healing energy that you seek.

When you get a lot of crystals at once, it can create a scenario that results in many superficial experiences that teach you little about the crystals' energies. Your attention becomes fragmented when you work with too many crystals at once, and you won't get a real sense of what each crystal does for you. Or maybe you will focus your attention on a few of your crystals, getting to know them well, while the rest of your crystals are ignored.

If you want the best experience with your crystals, focus on them one at a time. Take what you would have spent on many cheaper, little stones and buy one high-quality crystal instead. You will then be in a position to give one crystal your focused attention, which will make it easier to learn about its energetic capabilities and to see how its energies affect and heal you.

Taking the time to intimately work with your crystals helps you to clearly distinguish the differences in energy between them. Otherwise, if you work with several crystals at once without being able to distinguish their energies, you won't know which crystal is actually helping you. This also may result in a more complicated and extended healing journey for yourself because of all the different healing energies pulling at you at once. But if you work with one crystal at a time, you are able to learn all the different ways you can use each crystal's energies and how exactly these energies interact with you. And after you've gone through this process with each of your crystals, you will be in a better position to understand how to combine their healing energies in a more harmonic way.

Individually acquiring and working with crystals also allows you to develop a high-quality crystal kit. High-quality crystals have metaphysical energies that are more potent and beneficial to you in the long run. Instead of buying multiple cheap crystals for their separate metaphysical properties, take the time to find a high-quality crystal that resonates with you deeply on multiple levels. Over time you will find that you have a collection of crystals that you especially love looking at and that you profoundly connect with—crystals that you want to have with you for the rest of your life.

But how do you pick your crystals?

CHOOSING CRYSTALS BY POLARITY

You are attracted to crystals you need.

You may think you're attracted to a crystal only because of the way it looks, but that's not all. The patterning you see in the shape and color of the crystal is the physical representation of the patterning of energy within the stone. You are actually attracted to the crystal because beyond what you see are its energies, which you are resonating with. It's just that the first way you connect with the crystal is through your sight.

When I teach my introductory crystal workshop, I tell my students to avoid reading the names or metaphysical descriptions of the stones in the space. Instead, I ask them to look around and see which stones attract them. Even without reading the descriptions or having seen the stones before, every person invariably picks a stone they need. Solely through visual attraction, they will always choose a stone that resonates with an issue they are most concerned about.

Conversely . . .

You are repulsed by the crystals you need too.

Saying a stone is ugly is like saying a kitten is ugly. True, there are kittens on the more beautiful side of the scale, and others on the more ungainly, but no kitten is ugly. Likewise, a rock may not be as pretty as other rocks, but how can a rock truly be "ugly"? Yet sometimes this is how people react to certain crystals and stones.

So if you do have an immediate *ick* reaction to a stone, it means that energetically, you need it. And you probably need the stone you're repulsed by more than the stone you are attracted to! The reason why you find the stone to be ugly and repulsive is that it is resonating with the exact energies within you that need the most healing—but you are resisting it. You are avoiding healing this part of yourself, and it causes you to be visually and energetically repulsed by the stone. Otherwise, your reaction would be neutral, for you would neither favor nor dislike the stone. If you don't resonate with a stone, you simply won't react to it.

The funny thing is that everyone who works with a stone they are disgusted by eventually falls in love with it. Though it can take time, when people start experiencing how much their crystal supports and helps them, they begin seeing the crystal in a different way. Whereas before they resisted the energies that were produced by the stone, now they start to accept them. So as the person opens up to their healing, the stone begins to look beautiful to them.

You can try choosing a crystal using the polarity method the next time you walk into a crystal shop. Don't read the signs with the names and metaphysical descriptions of the stones. Just wander around and notice which stones you are attracted to and which stones you are repulsed by. Then return to the stones you noticed and read their metaphysical descriptions. You may find the information very enlightening.

EXPERIMENTING WITH CRYSTALS

You can take the polarity method one step further by conducting this fun crystal healing experiment: Without learning about its metaphysical properties, choose a durable stone that can be kept close to your skin. It can be a pocket stone, some crystal jewelry, or any stone that can be slept with. For the next month, work closely with your stone. After a month, look up the stone's properties and see if you have experienced any changes in your life relating to its metaphysical properties. You may find the results very interesting and a further affirmation of your connection with the crystals!

YOU DON'T ALWAYS
HAVE TO BUY CRYSTALS

As I have previously explained, certain minerals can be found only in specific places in the world. In order for these crystals to reach you, they go through a series of middlemen before they end up at a crystal shop or rock show. But going through retail channels is not the only way of procuring crystals. With the intuition you have developed because of the exercises in the book, you will find yourself connecting energetically with rocks you unexpectedly come across. As you have learned, you don't have to know the name of the stone or its specific metaphysical properties in order to work with it. So sometimes the best way of acquiring crystals is to pull them out of Mother Earth yourself.

Rockhounding is the amateur hobby of digging and collecting rocks from nature. It often involves traipsing through rugged landscapes, enduring harsh sunlight or inclement weather, and immersing yourself in absolute filth as you dig through dirt and mud. It is a hobby that is hard, exhausting, and totally fun. Getting an up-close and personal look at how minerals are found in the earth helps you see how crystals form, and experiencing how messy and difficult it can be to mine stones gives you a deep appreciation for those who do the work to bring crystals and stones to you. Following are a couple of great ways to begin your adventure into rockhounding.

I dug up this kunzite crystal on my first rockhounding trip.

First, there are many mines open to the public that allow you to dig for minerals or gems for a fee. Depending on the mine, this may mean you have access to water and sifting screens but have to pay for each bucket of dirt you sift through. Others will charge a day rate and allow you to sift through their piles of mine tailings (the leftover dirt from their mining operations) and collect any crystals they may have missed. At other mines, you pay for access to the site but have to bring all of your own equipment—including buckets, pickaxes, and water to loosen the dirt and clean your stones—but they let you dig and keep whatever you find. Though there are variations in how mines handle their fees, as well as the rules about what you can take from them and when, these are generally the different ways that fee-based mines like this work. Each mine will have specific kinds of minerals or kinds of rocks associated with it, depending on the geology of the land the mine sits upon. So while at one mine you might search for sapphires, another will have quartz, and another fossils. A website that lists these mining sites can be found in the resources section.

The second way to go rockhounding is to join your local rock and mineral club. Mineral clubs are found all over the world and are filled with passionate lovers of rocks. In addition to club meetings that showcase speakers giving talks on the scientific side of minerals, they put together field trips to go rockhounding. On these trips, clubs can get special access to private mines or permission to dig on land that belongs on someone's claim. In my experience, I have found these rockhounders to be quite generous when it comes to sharing their knowledge. They often have insider information about rockhounding in their area, and going on club field trips with them is a great way to learn the tricks of digging up crystals and stones. Though they may be dubious about your metaphysical interests, as long as you enjoy getting on your knees, digging in the mud, and getting as filthy as they do, your devotion to finding crystals will make you a worthy rockhounding companion.

While in rockhounding you actively set out to search for crystals, you can also accidentally stumble across stones while outdoors in nature or during your travels. Hiking on a trail or walking on a beach you may come across a stone that mysteriously enchants you. As you swim in a lake, a stone in the water may catch your eye. Or sometimes, you will be minding your own business and a rock will outright hit you.

Long before I knew I was a crystal healer or knew much about metaphysical stones, I went on a trip with my friends to swim in a river. Cooling myself off in the water, sitting quietly as the brisk current rushed around me, I felt something smack squarely into my thigh. Before I even pulled it out of the water, I knew that whatever it was was meant for me. It wasn't something that I had mindlessly picked up as I enjoyed the cool water, nor was it something I had searched for. I was clearly the target, as it hit my leg like a bull's-eye.

Out of the water I pulled a tan coral-like stone. For many years thereafter, I guessed that what I had was fossilized coral. But because I didn't know for sure, I couldn't research its metaphysical properties in crystal books. What I did know was that this stone was meant for me.

Much later I discovered the stone was fulgurite, a mineraloid created by lightning striking the ground, vitrifying the soil into a fused mass in the shape of lightning. Its metaphysical properties resonated with intense and immediate change, and looking back, I realize it was shortly after this stone came to me that I discovered crystals were my calling and embarked on my grand journey to become a crystal healer.

At the right place and moment, the crystal I needed most appeared to me.

The most important crystals in your life may not be crystals that you've bought. They may not be stunning or identifiable as a unique kind of stone. In fact, they may look quite ordinary to everyone else. But the most precious stones you will work with can be the stones that you come across in nature, given directly to you by Mother Earth.

Before you take home any crystals or stones you find in nature, you must respect the rules of whoever owns or has claims to the land. In the United States, rules vary from location to location. Many federally managed public lands allow the collection of stones for personal use, but you'll need to check with your local Bureau of Land Management (BLM) office for more specific information. Otherwise, if you're on private property, make sure you have permission from the person who owns the land to collect any stones found on it.

PERSONAL VERSUS GLOBAL CRYSTALS

I often get asked, "Is it okay for other people to touch your crystals?" The answer is, "It depends."

There are no fixed categories of stone ownership. But as you work with a stone, gain experience, and deepen your intuition, you'll find that you're better able to understand the stone's intentions, and who and where the stone wants to help. The fulgurite crystal that came to me at the river hit me in such a way that I knew it was meant only for me. This fulgurite crystal is my personal stone, meant only for me to work with. I don't let others touch it, but even if they did, it wouldn't "ruin" anything.

Over the years, I have developed a strong bond with my personal crystals. As I have worked with them, I have gotten to know their energies, as they have mine, and together we create a dynamic of energy. We know and have worked with each other's energetic nuances and this causes us to have a deeper resonance with each other. That's why my personal hematite works more strongly with me than others do. For though other hematites have the same base metaphysical energy, they don't have the same experience or bond with me as the hematite I work with at home.

Every once in a while, I might loan one of my personal crystals to my husband or a friend, but eventually the crystals always come back to me. Though others can benefit from the energies of my stones, like a favorite pair of broken-in shoes, my crystals will always "fit" me better.

You can also have crystals whose purpose is to be shared with others. Perhaps they are crystals to be shared within your family or crystals you use to foster community and cooperation at work. Or perhaps they are crystals you use with your healing work. When crystals are specifically chosen (or specifically want) to be used for helping others, they are global crystals whose energies are meant to be shared.

You may find that your crystals want to move from one category to another. Perhaps a personal crystal becomes a global crystal, or vice versa. Maybe you loan a crystal to a friend and realize that they actually belong together. Then, out of love, you may choose to release guardianship of the crystal to your friend. For sometimes you will be attracted to a crystal just because you are the right person to help the crystal get where it needs to go, to help bring it to the place where it can project its deepest healing.

CHOOSE FOR YOURSELF FIRST

Remember, the best way of helping others is to focus healing on yourself. And you do this by making yourself your priority and taking care of yourself first.

If you are going to work with crystals, choose them with intention and care. Invest in the crystals that support your own journey of healing; work with them, and allow them to help you.

As you heal, you will raise your own vibration. And because you are energetically connected to every other being in this world, raising your vibration means that you are raising the collective vibration of the world too. Thus, the act of healing yourself benefits everyone else.

So indulge in your own healing so that you may refill your own reservoirs of energy, and then keep going so that you can share the extra that spills over. Use the assistance of the crystals. They have been waiting eons to help you.

"As above, so below;
so below, as above."
—Hermes Trismegistus,
Emerald Tablet

Faden Quartz

A CRYSTAL HEALER'S ENCOURAGEMENT

As you have learned, crystals are not metaphysical robots. They are much more than that. They are energetic spirit guides made incarnate from the material body of Mother Earth.

Like your other relationships, your relationship with crystals is a two-way street. Just because you possess the arms and legs and have the power to move the crystals around does not mean you control the dynamic. Working with crystals is a partnership, a dance where your combined energies create another energy that is greater than the sum of its parts. It is an energy that strengthens and heals you but also raises the vibration of the world.

So congratulations on finishing this book. Your devoted presence with this information proves that you are indeed a crystal seeker with a sincere desire to understand crystal healing. You have opened yourself to crystalline understanding; all you need now is time, practice, patience, and awareness in order to take experience and turn it into wisdom.

Consider what you have learned here a template—a jumping-off point from which to build your experiences with the crystals. Heal yourself and raise your vibration with the crystals' help. And know that it is your unique energy, and the creativity that comes from it, that will push the frontiers of crystalline knowledge beyond what even I could ever know.

You are here on this planet for a special reason. So as long as you remember to open your heart and listen, the crystals will be here to support you. As long as your heart is sincere and true, the crystals will be here to guide you and help you to evolve in your journey.

The crystals have been waiting patiently for eons for your soul to awaken, but now the time has finally come.

The crystals are excited to embark on this journey with you.

CLOSING MEDITATION

Closing meditations bring an energy of completion. They mark the end of a chapter of experience and sanctify the process you have just gone through. In this case, you have gone on a grand journey learning about crystals, developing your intuition, and experiencing the alchemical result of these two elements synergizing into one.

This book began with an opening meditation to mark the beginning of your journey with the crystals. Now that you have completed all the chapters and exercises, it is time to mark the end of this journey. Though you may return often to this book and its information, it's important to recognize that you have just now completed one circle of experience in your education with the crystals.

This circularity has additional meaning within the symbol of the Ouroboros. As the snake bites its tail, it paradoxically marks both the end and another beginning of its journey. Though this circular movement is everlasting, each loop from head to tail can be seen as a completed segment within a greater scheme. So by recognizing this moment for yourself, you establish a point of perspective from which to view your own evolution within your grander spiritual journey.

The following closing meditation marks the completion of your journey through this book. To do this meditation, read the following words, take a deep breath, and close your eyes. Sit with the energy of the words until it completely settles into you. Then, when you are ready, open your eyes.

Thank you to the Crystals,

the Crystal Guardians,

and the Master Teachers of Light

for more deeply connecting me

to the crystalline worlds.

May I use my understanding

to heal myself, and thus heal others,

without ego, in humility

and in service to the world.

Amen/Namaste

CRYSTAL INDEX

The following are metaphysical properties for the stones recommended for exercise 5 (page 231). They are abbreviated summaries written from my own experience of working with these crystals and are meant to be used as broad guidelines for understanding their properties. The descriptions have been purposely written in a generalized and unspecific way in order to allow space for your experiences in the exercise to connect with the information presented here. If you wish to find more detailed information, you may elect to look at other perspectives written in crystal reference guides or internet resources. However, keep in mind that some descriptions are so vague that they won't say anything of significance or, when compared, will be widely disparate or even contradictory to one another. These are the descriptions to be avoided. Other authors will have clear and relatable descriptions that will touch and deeply resonate with you. You can learn more about how to figure out what information will be most helpful to you in the essay "Determining the Authenticity of a Crystal's Metaphysical Description" on page 240.

Please note that because of physical variances of minerals mined from different locations, your crystals may not look exactly like the ones shown in the following photos, but as long as your crystals have been correctly identified, they will have the same metaphysical properties as the descriptions indicate.

The crystals have been organized by color, starting from the crown chakra and ending with the root chakra.

MOONSTONE

Associated with yin energies including softness and femininity. It is a stone for pausing to be in the moment: for receiving energies or being in energies, rather than being in the process of an activity or a pursuit.

SELENITE

Connection to the energy of pure white spiritual light. This energy includes connection to your highest self and its connection to the highest spiritual wisdom. Associated with claircognizance. Also, the continual energy of cleansing and purification through white light.

AMETHYST

Amethyst is a gentle gateway into the spiritual worlds. It resonates with the subtle layer that borders the physical and ethereal dimensions. It makes spiritual energies more pronounced and tangible. It is also used to better understand new spiritual concepts or deepen knowledge of them.

LEPIDOLITE

Used to balance the energies of the mind, especially overactive ones. Extremely useful for anxiousness, as it tempers any tendency for the mind to split hairs and follow thoughts ad infinitum. Because it turns down the volume of the mind, it helps one to more clearly connect to the heart, emotions, and physical body and their respective wisdom.

SODALITE

A stone to stay true to your life's purpose. To help you make decisions that are aligned with your truest desires and dreams. Especially resonant with work and career. To support perseverance in discouraging times.

KYANITE (BLUE COLORED)

A stone to help boost communication and put information that is spiritual or emotional into verbal or other more tangible forms. Creates connections between the throat chakra and chakras above and below it. Helps to surface energetic information in a way that allows you to become conscious of it, as well as those you need to communicate with.

ANGELITE (AKA BLUE ANHYDRITE)

Connection to angels, transitioned souls, or spirit guides close to you. Helps connect one to transmitted information or messages from your loved ones in the spiritual realms. Intuitive information conveyed through physical sensations, kinesthetic movement, or sensate-based memories.

BLUE LACE AGATE

To assist communication flowing to and from you. Especially helpful when you are searching for the right words or the right way to begin what you want to say.

AQUAMARINE

"Cooling" energy helpful for toning down and softening anger or frustration. Takes the "edge" off of emotional communications, making them less sharp and pointed. Helps one to perceive the underbelly of situations and things. Associated with the water element.

RHODOCHROSITE

Inner child healing. Experiences and memories during childhood and youth needing to be healed. Often related to the most painful and tender wounds of childhood. A stone to support the strength that comes from healing these wounds.

RHODONITE

Understanding the importance of vulnerability when it comes to love. The relationship between vulnerability and connection with others. The value of openness and trust. Recollection of memories, some possibly long buried, of experiences related to being unexpectedly hurt. To allow negatively created emotional and psychic shields to come down so you may be healed.

GREEN AVENTURINE

Gentle examination of emotions in a compassionate and accepting way. To separate and sort out jumbled emotions and feelings into categories so that their context can be understood. The illumination of one's feelings in a soft way.

AMAZONITE

The stone of verbal integrity. Meaning what you say and saying what you mean. On a deeper level, it highlights any incongruity between your thoughts and actions. Thus, it focuses on any flakiness in your behavior and its consequences in your life. Also, the importance of integrity in relationship to your spirituality.

ROSE QUARTZ

See chapter 4, "The Essential Three," beginning on page 91.

MANGANO/MANGANOAN CALCITE

A stone helpful for those who always take care of others first and avoid taking care of themselves. To understand why one puts others before oneself. To support the establishment of an expression of love that is circulated in a balanced and healthy way. Particularly resonant with mothers and children seeking social acceptance.

MALACHITE

A stone to reveal and release suppressed emotions, often buried deeply. To be aware of the contours of what one is feeling. To understand the true source of why one feels the way one does. Especially resonant with males or others who have been conditioned to rationalize or ignore their feelings.

PREHNITE

For confidence and self-esteem. The ability to recognize one's contributions. The impetus to voice one's individuality and the determination to show it to the world. To feel wholly comfortable in taking up space to share one's personality with others.

PYRITE

Supports the physical manifestation of goals. Helps turn ideas into objects of concrete, tangible form. Assists with getting tasks completed.

TIGER'S EYE

Helps one understand one's desires and motivations in relation to one's ambitions; how this desire relates to one's life's purpose; and that the path to one's dreams is a meandering one, with many directional changes that create the experience needed to fulfill one's goals.

RED JASPER

A stone to boost courage and strength. To enhance determination and fortitude. Especially resonant with honoring the needs and wants of the physical body.

SMOKY QUARTZ

Brings additional light and energy into the physical body. Very supportive for those experiencing any kind of physical illness or duress that weakens the body. More deeply connects the soul to its physical existence. Helps to bring spiritual understanding of the experience of physical life.

OBSIDIAN (BLACK OR MOSTLY BLACK COLORED)

Supports you in cutting out what you no longer need in your life in a sharp and precise way. Can include things you may or may not be aware of. The removal of energy in an almost abrupt way, like quickly tearing off a bandage rather than slowly peeling it off to lessen the pain of removal.

BLACK TOURMALINE

See chapter 4, "The Essential Three," beginning on page 91.

HEMATITE

See chapter 4, "The Essential Three," beginning on page 91.

PHOTO INFORMATION

Information about the minerals' specific geographical origins, known as locality, has been shared, if known, using the original information provided with the specimens, without alteration. Locality information is of significant interest scientifically as it gives insight to the geology of the area the crystal originated from, while for mineral collectors it helps to determine rarity. The more detailed the locality information is, the more scientifically useful it is; it can also potentially make the mineral more valuable for collectors. Each listing also includes the crystal's dimensions (except in the case of tumbled stones).

When reading the below, it will be helpful for you to know a few mineralogical terms. A **matrix** is any rock material in which a fossil, crystal, or other material is embedded. **Pseudomorphs** are designated by the use of "after" in the mineral name and signify a crystal that once consisted of one mineral that was eventually replaced by a different mineral while still retaining its previous exterior form. Finally, in minerology, *provenance* denotes any information related to the history of the collection of a specific mineral specimen. Here "Provenance: Ex Rock H. Currier Collection" means the item has a history of once belonging to Rock Currier, a famous and significant mineral collector.

is not geologically considered a citrine, though it lends itself to citrine-like energies because of its color.

58   BERYL | Spargoville, Australia | 10.2 × 9.1 × 0.7 cm

60–61   LA PIETRA PAESINA (AKA RUIN MARBLE OR FLORENTINE MARBLE) | Florence, Italy | 10.2 × 7.1 × 0.7 cm

62   PINK PORPHYRY | Murchison Province, Western Australia, Australia | 27.1 × 6.3 × 9.7 cm

63   MALIGANO JASPER CABOCHON | Sulawesi, Indonesia | 3 × 3 × 0.5 cm | Cabochon cut by Gary Wiersema

64–65   QUARTZ AND MINOR CALCITE AND PYRITE | South Shetland Islands, Livingston Island, Antarctica | 9.2 × 8.9 × 6.2 cm

68   *Clockwise from top left:*
QUARTZ AND MINOR CALCITE AND
CHRYSOCOLLA | Congo | 8.6 × 9 × 4 cm
ANDRADITE GARNET | Mexico | 8.8 × 6.4 × 5.4 cm
LEPIDOLITE VARIETY "WATERMELON MICA" | Brazil | 8.2 × 5.4 × 0.7 cm
PHENAKITE | Nigeria | 1.9 × 1.4 × 1.1 cm
TOPAZ | 1.8 × 1.3 × 0.8 cm
SPINEL | 1.6 × 1.5 × 1.2 cm
EPIDOTE | Quetta, Balochistan, Pakistan | 4.9 × 4.3 × 3.1 cm
SODALITE
HEMIMORPHITE | Mexico | 7.6 × 6.3 × 4 cm

78   QUARTZ | Arkansas, U.S. | 10.6 × 2.9 × 3.5 cm

79   AMETHYST | 21.2 × 13.6 × 7.1 cm

80   ROSE QUARTZ | 8.3 × 8 × 5.3 cm

81   CITRINE | Shaba, Zaire | 7.7 × 4.4 × 2.9 cm

82   SMOKY QUARTZ | 5.7 × 2.1 × 1.8 cm

83   QUARTZ | Arkansas, U.S. | 10.1 × 6.5 × 4.2 cm

84   QUARTZ WITH SPECULAR HEMATITE | Musina, South Africa | 8.5 × 2.5 × 2 cm

85   QUARTZ WITH HEMATITE | Jinlong Hill, Guangdong Province, China | 11.2 × 8.7 × 9.4 cm

86   AGATE SLICE | 12.8 × 13.6 × 5.8 cm | Provenance: Ex Rock H. Currier Collection

87   OCEAN JASPER | Marovato Mine, Ambolobozo Peninsula, North West Coast, Madagascar | 5.6 × 3.3 × 0.4 cm

88   QUARTZ CHALCEDONY | Nasik, India | 7.1 × 4.8 × 3.5 cm

89   GOLD SHEEN OBSIDIAN (AKA MAHOGANY OBSIDIAN) | United States | 8.8 × 7.5 × 0.6 cm

90–91   *From left to right:*
BLACK TOURMALINE | Namibia | 6.3 × 2.5 × 1.5 cm
ROSE QUARTZ | 6.3 × 2 × 4.7 cm
BOTRYOIDAL HEMATITE | Morocco | 6.3 × 4 × 2.9 cm

93   BLACK TOURMALINE | Capelinha, Minas Gerais, Brazil | 14.5 × 9.7 × 6.3 cm

96   BLACK TOURMALINE IN QUARTZ CABOCHON | 3.1 × 2.2 × 0.5 cm

101   *From left to right:*
BLACK TOURMALINE | China | 4.1 × 3.6 × 4.2 cm
BLACK TOURMALINE | Brazil | 12 × 4.5 × 3.3 cm
BLACK TOURMALINE | Namibia | 5.1 × 4.9 × 5.3 cm

102   HEMATITE PSEUDOMORPH AFTER MAGNETITE | Payún Volcano, Altiplano del Payún Matru, Malargüe Department, Mendoza Province, Argentina | 6.9 × 6 × 5.2 cm

105   HEMATITE | Brumado, Bahia, Brazil | 3 × 2.1 × 0.4 cm | Provenance: Ex Rock Currier Collection

110   HEMATITE GEODE | Pilbara Region, Western Australia, Australia | 9.8 × 7.8 × 7.9 cm

115   BOTRYOIDAL HEMATITE | Morocco | 6.4 × 3.6 × 2.6 cm

116   LIMONITE AND HEMATITE PSEUDOMORPH AFTER MARCASITE (AKA PROPHECY STONE) | White Desert, Egypt | Approx. 8.7 × 1.2 cm to 13.6 × 3 cm each

123   HEMATITE WITH RUTILE | Novo Horizonte, Brazil | 3.7 × 3.5 × 0.5 cm

126   ROSE QUARTZ WITH DENDRITE INCLUSION | Brazil | 4.2 × 2.9 × 2.8 cm

129 ROSE QUARTZ GEODE (*left*) | Patagonia | 7.3 × 5.5 × 2 cm
PINK QUARTZ (*right*) | Pitorra Mine, Minas Gerais, Brazil | 5 × 3.8 × 2.6 cm Because these rare pink-colored quartzes have chemical formulas that differ from traditional rose quartz, they are not geologically considered rose quartz. But they are still energetically close enough to share rose quartz's purpose of manifesting divine love. In particular, the geode shapes provide an added focus of manifesting that love inward, toward one's self.

132 ROSE QUARTZ | 26 × 24.7 × 16.5 cm

135 RAINBOW LATTICE | Utnerrengatye (Rainbow Caterpillar) Mine, Harts Range, Northern Territory, Australia | 1.5 × 0.7 × 0.3 cm

144 LABRADORITE | 7.5 × 2.8 × 1.4 cm (*front*); 4.6 × 4.8 × 1.1 cm (*rear*)

146 AMETRINE | Anahi Mine, Santa Cruz Department, Bolivia | 9.5 × 2.9 × 4.1 cm | The color zoning in this stone occurs as a result of the trace hematite in the lattice changing oxidation states during the crystal's growth.

147 FIRE AGATES | Mexico | 1.1 × 0.8 × 0.6 cm (*top*); 1.4 × 1.2 × 0.6 cm (*bottom*)

149 *Outer circle, clockwise from top:*
CALCITE | Mexico | 15.4 × 10.8 × 9.2 cm
COBALT CALCITE | Congo | 7.2 × 6 × 4.2 cm
CALCITE | Huanggang Mine, Hexigten Banner, Ulanhad League, Mongolia Autonomous Region, China | 5.7 × 3.5 × 6 cm
CALCITE (BLUE ROUGH) | Mexico
SAND CALCITE | 6.7 × 2 × 1.9 cm
MANGANO CALCITE | Mangano, Peru | 5.8 × 3.4 × 3.1 cm
CALCITE (GREEN RHOMBOID) | Mexico | 5.8 × 2.2 × 2.1 cm
Inner circle:
CALCITES (ORANGE, CHARTREUSE, AND RED) | Mexico

150 TOURMALINE SLICES | 2.5 × 2.2 × 0.4 cm (*top*); 2.4 × 2.2 × 0.4 cm (*bottom*)

151 TOURMALINE SLICE | 3 × 3 × 0.3 cm

157 *Clockwise from top:*
ASTROPHYLLITE | Khibiny Massif, Kola Peninsula, Murmansk Oblast, Russia | 7 × 7.3 × 4.2 cm
CALCITE | Date Iron Mine, Hubei Province, China | 6.9 × 8.1 × 3.7 cm
COPROLITE | 3.6 × 1.5 × 1.4 cm
SPINEL IN MARBLE | Vietnam | 8.8 × 3 × 3.1 cm
WAVELLITE | Arkansas, U.S. | 7.9 × 5.4 × 5.8 cm

160 CITRINE RODS | Zambia | Approx. 3.4 × 0.6 to 5.4 × 0.6 cm each

161 RED PHANTOM QUARTZ | Zaire | 7.2 × 5.7 × 4.1 cm

162 *Top to bottom:*
BLACK TOURMALINE WITH CHRYSOCOLLA | 5.6 cm
BLUE LACE AGATE | 5.9 cm
ROSE QUARTZ | 7.2cm

163 *Top to bottom:*
OCEAN JASPER | 5.9 cm
LEPIDOLITE | 5.1 cm
QUARTZ | 7 cm
PINOLITH | 5 cm

164 QUARTZ | 6.6 × 4.5 × 2.4 cm

165 QUARTZ | Arkansas, U.S. | 7.7 × 3.6 × 2.5 cm

188 RED JASPER CONGLOMERATE (AKA JELLY BEAN JASPER) | Pilbara Region, Western Australia, Australia | 14.2 × 11.5 × 5.5 cm

189 CHIPBOARD RHYOLITE | La Paz County, Arizona, U.S. | 11.7 × 9.6 × 9.8 cm

190 RAINBOW OBSIDIAN CABOCHON | 9.2 × 9.2 × 1.4 cm | Cabochon cut by Kevin Lane Smith

191 FLUORITE WAND | 3.8 × 1 × 0.9 cm | Provenance: Ex Rock Currier Collection

192 AGATE EGG | 7.3 × 5.3 × 5.3 cm | Provenance: Ex Rock Currier Collection

193 TRAPICHE QUARTZ | Boyacá, Colombia | 3.5 × 2.3 × 0.6 cm

194 QUARTZ PLATONIC SOLIDS | Minas Gerais, Brazil | Approx. 2.8 × 2.8 × 2.8 cm each | Provenance: Ex Rock Currier Collection

195 QUARTZ VENTIFACTS | Thola Pampa, Potosí, Bolivia | Approx. 2.5 × 1.9 × 2 cm each

196–97 AGATE SNAIL (CHALCEDONY, OPAL, MOGANITE) | Dakhla, Oued Ed-Dahab-Lagouira, Western Sahara | 3.4 × 1.8 × 1.7 cm

202–03 MANGANOAN CALCITE | Manaoshan, Hunan Province, China | 14.5 × 5.3 × 3 cm

204–05 QUARTZ WITH PETROLEUM INCLUSIONS | Pakistan | 0.4 × 0.6 × 1.1 cm

208–09 QUARTZ SPHERE | 8.5 cm

220–21 CELESTINE VARIETY CHRYSANTHEMUM STONE | Liuyang County, Daxi River, Yonghe, Changsha Prefecture, Hunan, China | 7.9 × 7.2 × 3 cm

236 SMOKY QUARTZ | Argentière Glacier, Mont Blanc, Chamonix, France | 10.4 × 8.4 × 4.8 cm

237 PYRITE BALL | Hengyang, Hunan Province, China | 7.6 × 8.1 × 6.5 cm

238–39 GREEN FLUORITE ON QUARTZ | Fujian Province, China | 9.7 × 9.1 × 9.1 cm

242 SMOKY QUARTZ | near Zomba, Malawi | 9.6 × 3.4 × 2.5 cm

244–45 River-tumbled black tourmaline ring by As Above So Below

251 SMOKY QUARTZ HOPPER | Minas Gerais, Brazil | 7.3 × 5.6 × 2.6 cm | Provenance: Ex Rock Currier Collection

256 HALITE | Nacimiento, New Mexico, U.S. | 8 × 6.8 × 3 cm

257 SELENITE (rear) | Morocco | 21.3 × 3.7 × 3 cm
BROCHANTITE (front) | Milpillas, Sonora, Mexico | 3.3 × 3.2 × 1.2 cm

259 AMETHYST | Brazil | 11 × 7.2 × 4.1 cm (combined)

264–65 AMETHYST | Veracruz, Mexico | 19 × 17.7 × 4.7 cm

266–67 SPECULAR HEMATITE (bottom) | Michigan, U.S. | 22.2 × 17.8 × 0.9 cm
CALCITE, QUARTZ, AND HEMATITE (top; lower left) | Santa Eulalia District, Municipalidad de Aquiles Serdán, Chihuahua, Mexico | 7.6 × 7.4 × 2.6 cm | Provenance: Ex Rock Currier Collection

HEMATITE (TUMBLED) (top; upper right)

274 PYRITIZED AMMONITE (left) | Russia | 4.6 × 3.8 × 1.3 cm
SKELETAL PYRITE (right) | Purple Hope, No. 4 claim (Green Ridge), King County, Washington, U.S. | 6.5 × 5.1 × 3.6 cm

275 PYRITE RIVER STONE (left) | China | 5.6 × 5.2 × 5 cm
CUBIC PYRITE IN MATRIX (right) | Navajún, Spain | 4.2 × 6.8 × 3.8 cm

278 AMETHYST WITH PREHNITE | Goboboseb, Namibia | 3.9 × 2.7 × 2.4 cm

279 TECTONIC QUARTZ | Dalnegorsk, Russia | 6.8 × 6.4 × 6.1 cm

280 POLYHEDRAL AGATE | Paraíba, Brazil | 7.2 × 4.6 × 3.8 cm | Provenance: Ex Rock Currier Collection

281 JACINTO QUARTZES | Cortes de Pallás, Valencia, Spain | Approx. 1.7 × 1.1 × 1.1 cm each

282 TABULAR QUARTZ | Baixio Mine, Minas Gerais, Brazil | 18.9 × 15.8 × 1.6 cm

283 ETCHED QUARTZ | Baixio Mine, Minas Gerais, Brazil | 18.8 × 8.3 × 7.2 cm

284 TOURMALINE IN QUARTZ | Minas Gerais, Brazil | 5 × 3.3 × 2.6 cm

285 SMOKY QUARTZ | Piz Vial, Greina, Graubünden, Switzerland | 6.8 × 2.4 × 2.2 cm

286–87 SPODUMENE | Pala Chief Mine, San Diego, California, U.S. | 7.3 × 1.6 × 1.1 cm | Rockhounded by author

301 SELENITE STAR | Canada | 8.8 × 7.4 × 6.9 cm | Altar by Ako Castuera. Marble table by Nathan Hunt.

310–11 CUBIC PYRITE | Navajún, Spain | 19.7 × 10.4 × 10.2 cm

312–13 "SUGAR CUBE" BARITE WITH QUARTZ | Queenstake's Murray Mine, Zone 4, Level 175, Stop 13, Sugarbowl Pocket, Elko County, Nevada, U.S. | 11.4 × 7.4 × 8.9 cm

319 KUNZITE | Pala Chief Mine, San Diego, California, U.S. | 6.7 × 2.7 × 1.2 cm | Rockhounded by author

323 FADEN QUARTZ | Pakistan | 3.7 × 3.1 × 1.8 cm

325 SELENITE | Naica, Mexico | 6.6 × 5.2 × 2.2 cm | Ouroboros by Ako Castuera

ENDNOTES

PREFACE

10   **Much of the metaphysical jewelry:** Though *crystal* and *stone* have specific meanings
       geologically, for the purposes of this book the terms have been used interchangeably.

CHAPTER 3: THE IMPORTANCE OF THE QUARTZ FAMILY

67   **Any mineral that contains any amount:** "The Silica Family Tree," created by John
       Encarnacion [@a_geologist]. The more common, familiar varieties of minerals, mineraloids,
       and rocks made up mostly of silica. Chalcedony is fibrous quartz. Chert is microscopically
       granular (like sugar) quartz. Agate has curved layers of chalcedony; onyx has flat layers. Jasper is
       red chert (colored by iron oxides); flint is dark—usually black—chert. Coesite and stishovite are
       high-pressure varieties of silica. Cristobalite and tridymite are high-temperature, low-pressure
       varieties. Quartz is stable under "moderate" temperatures and pressures and at the Earth's
       surface. Instagram photograph, February 27, 2015, retrieved from https://www.instagram.
       com/p/zoZqRMLHmP/.

69   **Quartzes like these can become colored:** "Quartz," Mindat.org, n.d., accessed December
       28, 2017, https://www.mindat.org/min-3337.html.

69   **If you can see the crystals:** Also included in the micro-, cryptocrystalline quartz family are
       carnelian, plasma, sard, and heliotrope. See the website The Quartz Page at http//www
       .quartzpage.de.

70   **Sand, a nonrenewable resource:** UNEP Global Environmental Alert Service (GEAS),
       "Sand, Rarer Than One Thinks," March 2014. Accessed December 28, 2017, from
       https://na.unep.net/geas/archive/pdfs/GEAS_Mar2014_Sand_Mining.pdf.

71   **In 2016, researchers at the University:** "Eternal 5D Data Storage Could Record the
       History of Humankind," University of Southampton, News, February 18, 2016, https://www.
       southampton.ac.uk/news/2016/02/5d-data-storage-update.page.

71   **Each one-inch disk:** Based on a 3.1-megabyte plain text file. More precisely, the disk could
       store 121,770,116 copies of *War and Peace*, or 76,320 DVDs.

71   **Not only does the quartz glass:** Gabriel Bly, "The Future of Data Storage Is 5D,"
       Colocation America, Technology News, September 7, 2016, https://www
       .colocationamerica.com/blog/eternal-5d-data-storage.

71   **Most closely associated with Mesoamerican:** David Hatcher Childress and Stephen S.
       Mehler, *The Crystal Skulls: Astonishing Portals to Man's Past* (Kempton, IL: Adventures Unlimited,
       2008).

71   **Though the two cultural groups:** Lilou Mace, "Hunbatz Men: Mayan Elders, Prophecies,
       and Crystal Skulls," uploaded to YouTube December 11, 2013, https://www.youtube.com/
       watch?v=wJfnvXv9lzs.

72   **Current descendants of the ancient:** Chris Morton and Ceri Louise Thomas, *The Mystery
       of the Crystal Skulls: Unlocking the Secrets of the Past, Present, and Future* (Rochester, VT: Bear,
       2002).

72   **He was also responsible:** Esther Leslie, *Synthetic Worlds: Nature, Art and the Chemical Industry* (London: Reaktion Books/Chicago: University of Chicago Press, 2007).

72   **There, he would go on to research:** IBM, "Magnetic Stripe Technology," n.d., accessed December 28, 2017, https://www.ibm.com/ibm/history/ibm100/us/en/icons/magnetic/team/

73   **While conducting experiments:** Marcel Vogel, untitled manuscript, n.d., accessed December 28, 2017, http://marcelvogel.org/MarcelVogel.pdf.

73   **Vogel would go on to declare:** This quote from Dr. Marcel Vogel specifically references quartz cut to a precise design known as the "Vogel cut." In my experience, Vogel-cut crystals are extremely powerful, but unadulterated, natural quartz also works in the same way, just with less "laser-like" strength. Vogel, untitled manuscript.

CHAPTER 4: THE ESSENTIAL THREE

103   **Even though our Stone Age:** There is a possibility that these prehistoric Neanderthals from the Maastricht-Belvédère site in the Netherlands happened upon hematite near to them, but the largest known hematite deposit is roughly twenty-five miles away in Eifel. In these areas in Eifel with hematite deposits are Neanderthal sites that have stones from the Maastricht-Belvédère, lending some evidence to the connection of these two sites. W. Roebroeks, M. J. Sier, T. Kellberg Nielsen, D. De Loecker, J. M. Pares, C. E. S. Arps, and H. J. Mucher, "Use of Red Ochre by Early Neandertals," *Proceedings of the National Academy of Sciences* 109, no. 6 (2012): 1889–94.

103   **They then took great effort:** Ocher comes in a range of colors from yellow to sienna to burnt red depending on how the pigment was processed, but all ocher is derived from hematite.

103   **In addition to painting:** Michel Pastoureau and Jody Gladding, *Red: The History of a Color* (Princeton, NJ, Princeton University Press, 2017).

103   **This is why the ancient Greeks:** A student of both Plato and Aristotle, the Greek logician, botanist, ethicist, and all-around scholar Theophrastus gave hematite its original name, *aematitis lithos*, which means "blood stone," sometime between 325 and 300 BCE. Later an ancient Roman, Pliny the Elder, translated *aematitis lithos* to the Latin *haematites*, which means "bloodlike." "Hematite," Mindat.org, n.d., accessed August 31, 2017, www.mindat.org/min-1856.html.

103   **While the female sex:** Chris Knight, *Blood Relations: Menstruation and the Origins of Culture* (New Haven, CT: Yale University Press, 1995).

106   **Scientists have discovered:** The hypothesis that the inner core of the Earth was a solid ball of iron was made by Danish seismologist Inge Lehmann in 1940. It was later confirmed, in 1971, that the inner core is an iron-nickel alloy. (By the newest evidence, the composition of the inner core is actually 85 percent iron, 10 percent nickel, and 5 percent silicon.) Considering that women are the holders of many of the blood mysteries, I find it quite interesting this scientific theory originally came from a woman.

106   **This means *Mother Earth's*:** Most iron on the crust of the Earth is bonded with other minerals. Iron ores like hematite need processing in order to make pure iron. Free metallic iron is virtually unknown on Earth's surface.

107   **So while animals will run:** Maryann Mott, "Did Animals Sense Tsunami Was Coming?," *National Geographic*, October 2, 2018, https://www.nationalgeographic.com/animals/2005/01/news-animals-tsunami-sense-coming/.

107   **Information about an object:** Safi Marroun and Teresa McNulty, "Fingertips Increase Sensitivity to Touch: Modern Human," AskNature, August 16, 2017, https://asknature.org/strategy/fingertips-increase-sensitivity-to-touch/#.XLOLp-tKiL4.

114   **Grounding takes the overabundance:** In addition to the major chakras aligned with your spine, you have minor chakras, like those that are in your feet. The root chakra and the chakras in the feet have an important relationship with each other, as the foot chakras help transport the energy traveling down from your crown chakra down through to your root chakra. Then from the root chakra your foot chakras become the conduit to move the energy down into Mother Earth. It is a way of bringing down ethereal energies through your body and grounding them in the physical world.

127   **This is because love:** For more explanation of how love is not an emotion, see Karla McLaren, *Language of Emotions* (Boulder, CO: Sounds True, 2010).

CHAPTER 5: CRYSTALS, COLORS, AND CHAKRAS

138   **The number of these major:** Cyndi Dale, *The Subtle Body: An Encyclopedia of Your Energetic Anatomy* (Boulder, CO: Sounds True, 2009).

139   **Of all the systems:** The Vedic period lasted from 1500 to 500 BCE in the Indian subcontinent.

CHAPTER 6: HOW TO RECOGNIZE AND WHY TO AVOID ARTIFICIALLY ENHANCED CRYSTALS

173   **In every step of the process:** See the website of Jean-Noel Soni, www.topnotchfaceting.com.

173   **But this is actually a dishonor:** "Fluorite," Mindat.org, n.d., accessed May 30, 2017, https://www.mindat.org/min-1576.html. Fluorite also takes the shape of dodecahedrons, hexoctahedrons, and tetrahexahedrons.

174   **It's no coincidence:** Nicholas Kollerstrom, "Geometry of the Great Pyramid," Graham Hancock Website, January 6, 2009, grahamhancock.com/kollerstromn2/.

175   **Amethyst gets its purple:** Rock Currier, "Amethyst Specimens," Mindat.org, June 1997, https://www.mindat.org/article.php/905/Amethyst+Specimens.

175   **The amethyst is forced to change:** Kurt Nassau, *Gemstone Enhancement: Heat, Irradiation, Impregnation, Dyeing, and Other Treatments Which Alter the Appearance of Gemstones, and the Detection of Such Treatments* (Oxford: Butterworths, 1984).

179   **The atoms of metal:** "How Is Aura Rainbow Quartz Made?" Geology In, January 1, 1970, http://www.geologyin.com/2017/06/how-is-aura-rainbow-quartz-made.html.

184   **Quartz, emeralds, diamonds:** Kurt Nassau, *Gems Made by Man* (Radnor, PA: Chilton, 1980).

CHAPTER 8: HOW TO TAP INTO YOUR INTUITION

210   **Like the famous filmmaking:** This is a variant of a quote from Alfred Hitchcock, who said, "Drama is life with the dull bits cut out."

CHAPTER 10: CLEANSING AND CHARGING YOUR CRYSTALS

247   **But crystal building:** Alan Holden and Phylis Morrison, *Crystals and Crystal Growing* (Cambridge, MA: MIT Press, 1999).

249   **They, and the herbalists:** If you wish to learn more about the properties of sacred smudge plants and how to harvest them, seek an herbalist teacher or school that practices *ethical wildcrafting*. They will teach you about the plants and the criteria to follow in order to harvest plants ethically and sustainably.

252   **Of this water, 3.5 percent:** US Geological Survey, "How Much Water Is There on Earth?," n.d., accessed May 30, 2019, https://water.usgs.gov/edu/earthhowmuch.html.

252   **And all the water:** US Geological Survey, "The World's Water," n.d., accessed May 30, 2019, https://water.usgs.gov/edu/earthwherewater.html.

255   **In the world of metaphysical:** *Selenite* has different definitions in the geological versus metaphysical worlds. Gypsum is a mineral that comes in many forms from clear to fibrous, and from colorless to tinted in color, and historically geologists used to call only the clear and transparent form of gypsum selenite. But geologists no longer use this name, favoring the name *gypsum* for all forms of this mineral.

261   **It may need to be buried:** Something to consider if you're not actively using your crystals is to put them in a dark place for a while, since hiding out for a bit so they can enjoy their own energies is a nice energetic vacation for them, as it reminds them of when they were in Mother Earth.

CHAPTER 12: WAYS TO WORK WITH CRYSTALS

294   **This is why it is extremely:** On many crystal healing websites, black tourmaline is listed as toxic because of its aluminum content, but the International Gemstone Society says, "As long as you're not eating rock dust, toxicity from these stones is unlikely." Addison Rice, "Gemstone Toxicity Table," International Gem Society, n.d., accessed May 30, 2019, gemsociety.org/article/gemstone-toxicity-table/.

294   **Medical geology is an extremely niche:** Mindat.org., n.d.. Retrieved from https://www.mindat.org/.

SUGGESTED READING

Atlantis and Other Ancient Civilizations

Fingerprints of the Gods by Graham Hancock

Crystal Healing

The Crystal Trilogy by Katrina Raphaell

    Volume 1: *Crystal Enlightenment: The Transforming Properties of Crystals and Healing Stones*

    Volume 2: *Crystal Healing: The Therapeutic Application of Crystals and Stones*

    Volume 3: *The Crystalline Transmission: A Synthesis of Light*

Crystalline Illumination: The Way of the Five Bodies by Katrina Raphaell

Past Lives, Multiple and Alternate Realities

Seth Speaks: The Eternal Validity of the Soul by Jane Roberts

Sacred Geometry

The Ancient Secret of the Flower of Life vols. 1 and 2 by Drunvalo Melchizedek

Spiritual Integrity

The Four Agreements by Don Miguel Ruiz

RESOURCES

Crystals, Metaphysical Workshops, and Healing Sessions

PLACE 8 HEALING

place8healing.com

Place 8 Healing originally opened as a studio for my crystal healing practice but has since expanded to become a metaphysically based healing and wellness space with the purpose of vetting only the most heart-centered healers of integrity to share their wisdom and healing. Information on the retail shop, workshops, and events and the various healing modalities available at our Los Angeles space can be found on our website. Place 8 Healing also carries crystals for sale online, including the crystal set used for the exercises in this book, as well as a selection of fine metaphysical crystals and stones hand-picked by me for their metaphysical vibrancy and potency.

Crystal Healing Training

CRYSTAL ACADEMY OF ADVANCED HEALING ARTS

webcrystalacademy.com

Founded by Katrina Raphaell, this is the crystal healing school I trained in. If you are interested in learning about crystal healing to heal others, her school teaches the advanced techniques of laying stones. Courses available worldwide and online.

CRYSTALIS INSTITUTE FOR PERSONAL AND PLANETARY HEALING

crystalisinstitute.com

A crystal healing school led by Naisha Ahsian. She teaches techniques and approaches to the crystals that are different from those taught by my teacher at the Crystal Academy of Advanced Healing Arts. Though I am not familiar with the specifics of what she teaches, I deeply respect her written work, as through her writings she expresses her deep connection, integrity, and commitment to the crystals.

Crystal Meditations

INSIGHT TIMER

insighttimer.com

This free meditation app is available on Apple and Android and includes thousands of different meditations from various teachers. Crystal meditations led by me can be found on this app under my name.

Fee Mining Locations

ROCKTUMBLER.COM

rocktumbler.com/blog/fee-mining-and-digging-sites/

If you are interested in digging for gems and minerals, this webpage (from a site focused on the lapidary art of rock tumbling) lists various fee mining sites, mainly in the United States.

INTERNATIONAL GEM SOCIETY

gemsociety.org/article/gemstone-toxicity-table/

Unfortunately, there isn't a comprehensive listing of minerals and their toxicity when used in gem elixirs, but information can be gleaned from other mineral-based disciplines like that of gemstone cutting. This webpage lists the toxicity of various gemstone materials, though it does not explicitly specify if the toxicity is the result of normal handling, physical cutting of the material, or ingestion. For gem elixirs, pay the most attention to any entries that mention hazards with ingestion, solubility, or any other reaction to liquids.

AS ABOVE SO BELOW

asabove8sobelow.com

The project that started my journey toward becoming a crystal healer, As Above So Below is a metaphysical fine jewelry line made in accordance with fair-trade, ecological, and ethical principles. All pieces are intentionally designed with my understanding and experience as a crystal healer to support the wearer's healing.

MINDAT.ORG

This site is the ultimate resource for mineralogical information online. This nonprofit organization's mission is to advance the world's understanding of minerals by providing a comprehensive database of information about minerals and their localities, along with specimen photos. Information is uploaded all over the world by volunteers and then verified by geological experts. It's my go-to site for scientific information about the geological properties of individual minerals.

THE-VUG.COM

the-vug.com/educate-and-inform/rock-and-gem-clubs/

The-Vug.com is the self-described "home for all things mineralogical online." Their website has the most comprehensive listing of rock and mineral clubs in the United States, sorted by region and by state, along with a listing of a few international organizations.

ROCKANDMINERALSHOWS.COM

Many rock and mineral shows are sponsored by local clubs who bring in outside dealers to sell minerals and mineral-related goods. This site has an exhaustive listing of open-to-the-public shows, which can be sorted by state and date.

XPO PRESS

xpopress.com/show/countries

Xpo Press is known for being the publisher of the printed show guides for all major gem shows in the United States. Their webpage also lists a calendar of gem, mineral, fossil, and jewelry shows outside of the United States.

ACKNOWLEDGMENTS

A shaman's job is to safely guide a person through alternate realities, to lead them through myriad unfamiliar and sometimes treacherous psychic adventures, and to assist people in their goals of self-fulfillment. Bridget Monroe Itkin, thank you for being my publishing shaman, adeptly guiding me through what was, for me, the strange, alien world of bookmaking. This book would not have been everything it was meant to be without your deft skill navigating me and this book through it all.

To the rest of the team at Artisan Books: Lia Ronnen, Carson Lombardi, Nina Simoneaux, Michelle Ishay Cohen, Jennifer K. Beal Davis, Nancy Murray, Allison McGeehon, Theresa Collier, and Amy Michelson. How wonderful it has been to work with such a group of strong and powerful women. Every step of the way, each one of you has shown me your dedication to excellence and your commitment to producing the best book possible, and the results show.

To my agent, Meg Thompson: Thank you for understanding what this book was meant to be, and for always having my back.

Rock Currier: "Agates? You like agates???" you facetiously sneered as you pretended to look down your nose. In your sly jest you showed me that you were not one of those high-end mineral snobs, but a true lover of rocks. We all sorely miss your physical presence, but I hope to help keep the memory of you alive through some of the beloved minerals that were in your collection that are now presented in this book. May your contributions to mineral knowledge and your infamous humor and mirth be never forgotten.

Alfredo Petrov: I hope this acknowledgment doesn't ding your street cred with your fellow geologists. Thank you for always explaining all my geological questions and never treating me as a lesser just because I'm one of those "healy-feelies." I have always appreciated your passion and joviality (as well as all the hints on where to get the good finds).

To Kristin Pinnow, Rosie Pineda, and Linlee Allen: Place 8 Healing would not have been without your help. Each one of you has played an important role in helping me develop and grow the space that created the foundation for this book. And to the clients, supporters, and friends of Place 8 Healing: Thank you for loving the crystals and being true seekers of love and healing.

The photos of the crystals would not have been as beautiful had it not been for the production help of Dennis Middleton, Ako Castuera, Rob Sato, Beth Katz, Junzo Mori, and the help from the team at Samy's Camera Pasadena including Juan Gonzales, Jason Lyman, and Andy Sanchez. And thank you to Miles Wintner for creating the illustrations for this book, Amir C. Akhavan for allowing us to adapt your drawing of the quartz structure, and Yudi Ela for the photograph that exquisitely captured the beauty of a crystal healing session.

To Patricia Kaminski and Richard Katz: For being such great teachers of Mother Earth's plant beings and for being such role models of dedication and integrity in teaching the energetic arts.

To my crystal sisters Antoinette Aurell, Tedra Baymiller, and Tara Hofmann: I am so thankful that our journey to become crystalline healers happened together. I am forever thankful for our companionship and support of each other. And to Katrina Raphaell for being our teacher and initiating our understanding and awareness of the crystalline worlds.

To the catalysts on my journey to my purpose, Christina Chungtech and Jean Noel-Soni: Thank you for being important players in helping me discover my life's purpose.

To all my awesome friends for their continued love and support. I love you guys.

Thank you to my plants and animal family, with special regard to my desk kitties who while I was in the convolutions of writing constantly reminded me about taking in the pleasures of now.

To Mother Earth, for giving us a place to live and providing us with all the materials we need to become self-fulfilled. Thank you for sharing your crystal beings to teach us and being so patient and loving of us silly humans.

To my mentor, Marsha Utain: There are no words to adequately express my gratitude for your guidance and help. What I have been able to become is because of you. Thank you.

And last but definitely not least, to my husband, Marc Brown: I never expected to find a life partner, but I now realize why the Universe put us together. None of my work with the crystals could have happened without your love and support. And though I am the author of this book, you are as much responsible for getting the information out about the crystals as I am. Thank you for always being my rock. I love you.

INDEX

Page numbers in *italics* refer to photo captions.
For uncaptioned crystals, see Photo Information (pages 333–36).